The
Hope
that is in
Us

Members and Friends
of
St. John's Episcopal Church
Naples, Florida

ISBN: 9781097206575

St. John's Episcopal Church
500 Park Shore Drive
Naples, Florida 34103
(239) 261-2355

Printed
by
Kindle Direct Publishing

This book was written for
all who seek hope.

"… in your hearts revere Christ as Lord.
Always be prepared to give an answer
to everyone who asks you
to give the reason for the hope that you have.
But do this with gentleness and respect…"
1 Peter 3:15-16 (New International Version)

PREFACE

I remember spending periodic summers on my grandparent's farm in West Virginia as a young boy. I'd help plant and weed the garden and, of course, eat the wonderful produce, feed the chickens, gather the eggs, pick up fresh milk from the local dairy farm and do a ton of work throughout the day. One of my favorite pastimes was to listen to my grandpa tell stories on the back porch overlooking the meadow below us. He shared about his life during the Great Depression, working at the glass factory, how to clear a hornet's nest from a tree and I could go on and on.

I loved hearing those stories and still enjoy listening to people share about their journeys. "The Hope that is in Us" is a collection of inspiring stories of God moving in people's lives. This book celebrates that God still touches people in miraculous ways, both simple and profound. It will also give you hope that God can still transform your life and the lives of all you know who need him.

Be blessed as you read these stories and realize the tales we share can change lives. I encourage you to share your story because people want to hear it and be touched by God through you!

Father Joseph Maiocco
Rector, St. John's Episcopal Church

Don't you love a good story?
This book is chock full of good stories.
Better yet, these stories are true.

INTRODUCTION

This project began out of our Lenten devotion "40 Days of Decrease." Through that book, author Alicia Britt Chole took us on a deep dive into John's story of Jesus's journey from Bethany to Jerusalem, from the cross to the tomb, from the garden of the resurrection to the Father's throne. Like John, we were filled with wonder, joy and thanksgiving.

The storytellers you will encounter in this volume have written to remember, to reflect, to memorialize, to witness and to encourage you. Some start "on a dark and stormy night," some with how they first fell in love with Jesus, some with when they fell in close step with Jesus, some with when they stumbled, but Jesus helped them get back on their feet. They all end in wonder, joy, and thanksgiving.

As you read these stories, look for shared experiences. Have you ever experienced loss, grief, disappointment, danger, despair? What about confusion, doubt, burn-out, emptiness, disconnect, loneliness, paralysis, fear? How did these storytellers move beyond? Let them tell you....

SPOILER ALERT: God showed up! He broke through! He got their attention—not just once, but time and again! And what a difference that made in their lives!

Their stories will move you and hopefully encourage you to tell your stories. What a difference you will make in someone's life. Prepare to be amazed!

Donna Beecher
Senior Warden, St. John's Episcopal Church

CONTENTS

CHAPTER 1

Open the Door

"Here I am! I stand at the door and knock.
If anyone hears me and opens the door, I will come in and
fellowship with that person, and they with me."
Revelation 3:20 (New International Version)

My father was very smart and a good provider. He could always find something a little better than what we had. I would always see him praying every morning before he went to work. He came home when I was four years old and told my mother that the four of us—my parents, my eight-year-old sister and I—were leaving the Ukraine to seek freedom. She only had two hours to pack.

We got on a train, but it was 1942 during the war. The track was bombed, so we had to take to the woods and walk. If we were found, most likely we'd be sent to Siberia. Signs of battle and bloodshed were all around us. We slept on the ground, but if it rained, it seemed like we never got wet. The LORD protected us with His umbrella.

One night, we were in an open field when a bright light suddenly appeared. With no trees to shield us, my parents covered my sister and me with their bodies. Thank God it was not a Russian tank. We had sacks of bread and bitter water for our meals. My father fished or found some work to get us more food. When I contracted diphtheria, he searched for medicine long after curfew, but when he finally found it, it was too late. It didn't work, and I was turning blue. I had an emergency tracheotomy without anesthesia. It didn't look as if I would make it. But I did.

We safely reached the camps for displaced people in Germany where we'd stay for the next four years. Seven and a half additional years and two countries later, we reached the United States. My earthly father had brought me as far as he could on the journey, but it would take my Heavenly Father to help me find freedom...

Some years later, I was living in Paducah, Kentucky with my husband and children. As an OB-GYN, Paul was "married" to his work. I hardly saw him, and he didn't seem to need me. Our children's English was better than mine. I couldn't help them with their reading or writing and didn't want them to pick up my accent. I felt like a failure as both a wife and a mother and contemplated ending my marriage.

That's when I met a beautiful woman in a beauty shop. She was so vibrant and had such joy that I was attracted to her. I wanted what she had. When we began to talk, I was surprised to learn that she had terminal breast cancer.

She sensed that I needed something and asked Paul and me to a meeting at the home of a friend of hers. Her friend was an heiress of a Coca Cola business. I really just wanted to go see her house. I wasn't that interested in what the meeting was about, but we went.

At the meeting, Ben Hayden gave his testimony. He'd been a successful lawyer and newspaper editor with his marriage on the rocks when Billy Graham came to town. He said to his wife, "Charlene, let's go just to see people making fools of themselves." At the closing of the service, instead of laughing at the "fools," his wife went forward, and Ben followed her. They both accepted Christ. He changed their lives and saved their marriage.

I thought, "If God could do that for him, maybe he could do that for me."

I remembered Ben Hayden reading Revelation 3:20 where Jesus says, "I stand at the door and knock. If anyone hears me, then I will come in and fellowship with that person and they with me."

"Well, LORD," I said, "here I am. I confess that I've been trying to run my life in my own power and making a mess of it. If there is such a thing as you coming into my heart, my heart is open."

When I got up from my knees, I was filled with joy. It was indescribable. I went to every mirror in my home and looked at myself. I felt like I was smiling from one ear to the other. For the first time, I truly felt that God loved me, and it is that Truth that finally set me free to be free forever (Galatians 5:1).

Jeanne Price

CHAPTER 2

Trust in the Lord

*"Trust in the Lord with all thine heart
and lean not unto thine own understanding.
In all thy ways acknowledge him,
and he shall direct thy paths."*
Proverbs 3:5-6 (King James Version)

My grandmother always prayed for me. Toto (pronounced Tutu) prayed silently at every meal. My family seemed embarrassed, but even then, I revered her. When I was six, the woman I was named after died in her sleep. My mother was crying when she told me, and I remember thinking, "Why would you cry? She's with Jesus!"

Neighbors took me to the Episcopal church when I was a child. When I was an adult, something in my heart yearned to return. At twenty, I joined the Episcopal church, and when the bishop put his hands on me, I knew the Holy Spirit had come into me.

After I married, our three-month-old daughter was infected with TB. When a post-treatment x-ray revealed no

5

infection or scaring whatsoever, her doctor said, "This child doesn't have TB. She's never had TB," yet all prior X-rays revealed that one lung had been completely infiltrated!

Although grateful for our daughter's healing, I hesitated to trust God with anything really important, fearing I'd lose faith if things didn't turn out well. Then, our friend Bob, a young husband with small children, was hit by a truck. When I mentioned Bob was in terrible shape, my backyard neighbor said, "Get Marilyn's church to pray. When her church prays, people get healed."

At Marilyn's Wednesday prayer service, I was suddenly engulfed in a cone of magnificent rosy-gold light that extended far beyond the ceiling of the parish hall. I felt the love of God pour into me, and I sobbed. When Bob went home to God, I did not lose my faith. Awash in God's Love, I truly found it.

In the idyllic community where we began to raise our children, we had a minister who had gone to all the right prep schools and colleges. He was grandson of a bishop and head of the "right" church. One year, the pastor and some men from an African-American storefront church, members of the local ministerial association, came to our pastor and said, "You need to let us pray that the Holy Spirit will be part of your life and ministry." When they prayed for our minister, he experienced the baptism of God's Holy Spirit. It changed his life and through his life, our church.

Each summer, our family water skied. One day our daughter fell directly in the path of our neighbor's boat. He failed to see her as he raced toward his dock. "LORD, You saved her once! She's Your child!" I prayed. Inexplicably, our neighbor abruptly shut off his motor. Seeing our daughter, he blanched.

"I didn't see her! I don't know why I turned off the motor!" He said. He may not have known, but I surely did!

After years in a wonderful community with a great church and great schools, my husband got a job at one of the far ends of the Earth. I was not happy to say the least, but within weeks I was a member of a powerful local prayer group of old ladies. God told me then, "Feed my sheep. Feed my *old* sheep."

I began inviting widows to dinner. Finally, we found a house in a desirable neighborhood and moved in. When the moving truck left, my new next-door neighbor came to my backdoor.

"I just want you to know I've been praying for you, and I know that the Lord wants you here. This is where you're supposed to be," she said. We lived there for thirty years.

When my husband developed dementia, he and I moved to a multi-level care facility, and God said to me, "I am with you in this place." When Skip passed away, I began a ministry to older people which continues to this day. I am grateful to say, "He's still directing my paths."

Ann Gibson

CHAPTER 3

Life's Miracles

"For we know that if the earthly tent
we live in is destroyed,
we have a building from God, an eternal house in heaven,
not built by human hands."
2 Corinthians 5:1 *(New International Version)*

My husband and I were married for thirty-eight years, the last three years of which his health declined due to a very rare form of cancer—chronic myeloid leukemia with five genetic mutations. His doctors estimated that only two hundred people had ever been diagnosed with this form of cancer. At that time, my husband was one of only two dozen with the diagnosis in the world.

What an uplifting experience it is to look at life as a miracle, to view each day as a gift. My husband was told he had five months. He managed to survive thirty-five during which we experienced much pleasure together exploring the wonder of God's presence, the meaning of life and our role in it and how to provide for others as we prepared for separating. We talked about art and literature, the beauty of nature, the gifts of the life around us including the blessing of our large blended family of my four and his three children and our grandchildren.

We had always valued our Episcopal faith, but during this time, we came closer to our church and relied more on its support. Believing even more strongly in its sacraments, we regularly sought communion. When we were no longer able to get out, our friend Andrew Smith, a wonderful man and retired Connecticut bishop, graciously came to our home and invited me to participate fully as his assistant in the experience.

Before my husband passed away, we discussed how he might be able to share his presence after death. He might be able to turn a light or the television on. We dismissed these both as being easily explained away by natural phenomenon. While they may very well have been just what we were looking for, we concluded that we couldn't be certain, so we shouldn't count on either of these as sure signs.

"Well, then what do you think you could do to let me know about your ability to stick around?" I asked.

"I know what I'll do," he replied. "I'll ring the doorbell."

"Honey, you know the doorbell doesn't work anymore," I said.

"That won't be a problem," he said with a smile. "When you hear it, be sure to look, but don't expect to see anyone." Situated on a hill, our shingled Nantucket-style home had a wrap-around veranda and a circular drive with clear sight lines of the street from both the back and the front.

I was with my husband in the hospital when he passed away. I climbed into the hospital bed beside him when I knew he was breathing his last breath. We embraced and said, "I love you so much." As we said our farewells, we spoke our hope of being reunited.

Five days later, I was in the house by myself when the doorbell rang loud and deep, twice. I went to the front door, opened it and looked out. There was nobody there. I raced to open the back door. No one was there either.

I returned to the front door. Straight ahead, a butterfly hovered at the column to my right, and a dragonfly hovered at the column to my left. As I stepped out, the butterfly flew directly past me over to the dragon fly. After a moment, the dragonfly crossed to the other column. From out of nowhere, a warm, delicious breeze swept over me.

Carol Schaller

CHAPTER 4

Knowing Our Father

"Yet those who wait for the Lord will gain new strength;
they will mount up with wings like eagles.
They will run and not get tired,
they will walk and not become weary."
Isaiah 40: 31 (King James Version)

I grew up in Baltimore.

Early on, I recognized my mother was obsessed with alcohol. My father went to great lengths to try to stop her addiction without letting anybody know it existed. He shielded me as best he could, but that left little time for much else.

I never really knew my father.

I went off on my own, and found a group of friends at a church. I listened as the rector gave his sermons. He spoke of God watching over each one of us. That sounded pretty good, but then he warned us not to sin or we would go to Hell. After that, I figured I should do whatever I could to stay under God's radar so He wouldn't zap me.

I didn't really know my Heavenly Father either.

Many years passed before I found my loving wife, Ellie. Together, we found an active Episcopal Church that introduced us to Cursillo, a weekend course on Jesus Christ, and our eyes were opened.

We discovered that God's love and compassion are boundless. He is slow to anger and eager to forgive. He gives lavishly and pleads with us to take the very best. He always has time, and He always understands. Truly knowing God, who in their right minds would ever choose to stay under His radar?

Through Jesus Christ, both Ellie and I became acquainted with our Heavenly Father, and the more we knew Him, the more we wanted to be like Him.

As a result, both Ellie and I have enjoyed being on numerous Cursillo teams where we helped others get to know Christ in depth. When we came to Naples and St. John's, we found St. Matthew's House, a home for the homeless, and a chapter of Stephen Ministry, a program of Christian encouragement, where we worked helping people with the bumps in the road.

Through daily prayer, Bible study and small group discussions, our Heavenly Father gives us new strength and empowers us to mount up with wings like eagles. Thanks be to God!

Tony Leigh

CHAPTER 5

Love Binds Everything

"Put on then, as God's chosen ones, holy and beloved,
compassionate hearts, kindness, humility, meekness, and
patience, bearing with one another and, if one has a
complaint against another, forgiving each other;
as the Lord has forgiven you, so you also must forgive.
And above all these, put on love,
which binds everything together in perfect harmony."
Colossians 3:12-14 (English Standard Version)

My sister was killed by her husband many years ago.

I thought I had put to rest the pain associated with her death. I had gone through a healing experience that brought me peace, removed the sadness and all the other emotions associated with her death, or so I thought.

But the Lord wasn't done with me yet. More healing was in store.

Recently, my aunt showed me a request on social media from someone wanting to know more about her family. The person only knew the last name of her estranged family.

"Who is this?" I asked when I read the post, looking at my aunt.

"It's your sister's granddaughter, Shannon," she said.

Bam! Pain and sorrow struck again. I was so angry at my aunt that I left the house. As I walked, I grumbled.

"I dealt with this already! Leave things alone! Stay out of my business! Don't open Pandora's box!" Even as I said those words, I could not ignore the reflection exercise in my Lenten study that advised against "speeding past sorrow," and called to "honor the losses in your life . . . slow down and be present to your emotions" (*40 Days of Decrease*, Day 6, by Alicia Britt Chloe).

Honoring the loss of my sister, I called her granddaughter, and a deeper healing began.

Shannon cried and gave praise to God when she heard my voice. For over thirty years, she had searched for her family. When no one came forward, she questioned God, but now she rejoiced that her prayers had been answered. We talked and shared many thoughts. I was unaware how much my sister's death had such ricocheting effects on future generations.

Shannon and I are on our way to healing, to growing in God's love and building our relationship in the name of Yvonne—sister, mother, grandmother.

Jeannette McDonald

CHAPTER 6

Embraced by a Mighty Wind

"Suddenly a sound like the blowing of a violent wind
came from heaven
and filled the whole house where they were sitting."
Acts 2:2 (New International Version)

I have always known that God is with me, but one day He showed up in a way that assured me of His tender love for me in a way as never before.

Late one March afternoon almost ten years ago, I was sitting alone in my family room with my back to the main part of the house. My mind was spinning with all the controversy that took place in my home on a daily basis. I felt alone and in despair.

Nobody was in the house, but me. No television was on, not even a radio. I believe that the front door was locked because I never left it unlocked.

All of a sudden, I heard the front door open and shut, so I called my daughter's name, thinking she'd returned home early from work, but there was no answer.

As I continued to listen, I heard the sound of a

17

gigantic wind coming from behind me. I was engulfed in a strong, warm embrace which felt so absolutely fabulous that I never wanted it to stop. I felt completely safe, perfectly peaceful and totally loved.

Then just as quickly as it came, it was gone.

A few weeks later, I was sitting in a Lenten study on a Wednesday night. My priest, Father Joe, was sitting to my right. The book we were studying lay open in front of me. We took turns reading from the text. When we came to one portion of the lesson, I caught my breath.

"When the Holy Spirit comes into your life, it comes with the sound of a huge wind."

I read the words again and again. They began to blur as my eyes filled with tears.

Why me? I asked myself. *Why had God so honored me?* Instantly, deep within me I heard, *Why not you?*

After all, I am God's beloved child whom He embraced with the mighty wind of His Holy Spirit. I felt then, and I continue to feel, so very blessed.

Barbara Youngs

CHAPTER 7

God Has a Plan

"'For I know the plans I have for you,'
declares the LORD,
'plans to prosper you and not to harm you,
plans to give you hope and a future.'"
Jeremiah 29:11 (New International Version)

My presence on this earth was an oops!

My sister was thirteen years older than me. Need I say more? When she left for boarding school, then college, my parents no longer had a built-in babysitter, so they hired me a nanny.

My Miss Horn loved her Jesus and she said so. She taught me prayers and songs I still say and sing. I attended our town's Episcopal Church and was confirmed. I sang in the choir and was Mary in the Christmas play, so I guess you could say I was "churched."

Miss Horn went to another church. I never understood why until I got older, for in my heart she was my mom. She was always there. We talked, fished, went on walks, watched TV, played cards, and ate meals together for twelve years.

My seventh summer, I was sent to camp for two months—a camp I would attend two months every summer for nine years. When I was old enough to go to boarding school, I was sent away and my wonderful Miss Horn, my nanny, was fired.

I was heartbroken.

I stopped going to church. We had chapel at boarding school, but there was no teaching of the Bible. With all the traveling from our summer and winter homes, boarding school and summer camp, I never made true friends. Everyone was an acquaintance. There were times I felt very alone and pretty much an outsider everywhere I went. That changed when I went to college.

It was there I met my guy. He and his family became my family. His mom called me "her daughter she never had." We were like two peas in a pod. I learned so much from her and was honored to take care of her before she passed to be with the Lord.

Miss Horn left her love of the Lord within me. What a gift! My guy's mom became mine and helped nurture that love. Writing this brings tears, but even as I yearn to see these two godly women again in heaven, I realize that God did not leave me comfortless.

Six years ago, I received a call out of the blue from an aunt I'd never met, and we hit the ground running. She tracked me down through my nephew—thank God. Her husband is a pastor, and their vibrancy and love of God is so apparent, it is contagious!

Today, I know that nothing about me is or ever was even remotely an oops. God planned every minute detail. He graciously brought these and so many other extraordinary people into my life. I pray that I can show to others the love He's given me.

A Grateful Believer

CHAPTER 8

With All Your Heart

"I know the plans I have for you….
You will seek me and find me
when you seek me with all your heart."
Jeremiah 29: 11,13 (New International Version)

I believe God had plans for me even before I was a twinkle in my Dad's eyes. Somehow, growing up in a happy but not particularly religious family, I always believed in God.

My earliest recollection of God being talked about occurred when I was a skinny six or seven-year-old changing out of my wet swimming suit in an old wooden bathhouse, as my aunt, a Christian Scientist visiting from far off California, taught me the Lord's Prayer!

Learning about the pilgrims was all I remember from the eighth grade confirmation classes in the Congregational Church.

After I married Phil, a cradle Episcopalian, I slept in while he went off to church.

Fast Forward. Three children later, all baptized and in church with us every Sunday, I began to deal with Jesus. Who was He, anyway? I looked for Him first in the public library. (I didn't find him.) Our priest gave me a little better direction, and eventually I accepted Jesus as Lord. I was confirmed in the Episcopal Church and God became my part-time consultant.

Fast Forward. A new couple at the coffee hour talked about Jesus as though they really knew Him! Strange! Not long after several other strange "God incidences." I found myself with Phil, on my knees on someone's living room floor. A truly born-again moment. God became my full-time boss. A few years later, Cursillo in the mountains of New Mexico. A heavenly spiritual high!

Fast Forward. St. John's, Naples. Children all leaving the nest. A witnessing community reaching out to me. A twenty-year journey of regular church involvement and attendance. But there were many weeks when I never thought about God from Sunday to Sunday. God had again become my part-time consultant.

Unhappy with my faith journey, I asked a good friend, Joan Warren, what I might do. Joan organized a handful of women who committed with us to a weekly morning meeting with the goal of growing spiritually. At first there was no difference in my life except I had to admit to the group that God had again been pretty much forgotten. But then it changed.

One of the women in the group said that she would get up every morning at 6:00 a.m. for the coming week to pray for me if I would get up at 6:00 a.m. to spend some quiet time with God. It was one of the most touching gifts I've ever received, and it changed my life.

Quiet time with God is now a daily part of my life, and "Grouping," as we call it, has made the biggest difference in my spiritual journey. Support, prayer, encouragement, and love for one another—all these in abundance. But most importantly, my needing to be honest with the group has kept me honest with myself.

Recently, God has been speaking to me powerfully through his Word. The words "I have plans for you" keep going through my mind (Jeremiah 29:11). Until now, however, I never saw Jeremiah 29:13, just two lines later, "You will seek me and find me *when you seek me with all your heart.*" And that has become my verse.

The more time I spend seeking Him, the more I realize what an awesome God He is and how unbelievably great is His love for me, for us. God has been filling me with incredible joy and gratitude. What I seek is more of God because I know He has plans for me, plans to prosper me and not to harm me. And whatever His Plans are for me, He will be with me every step of the way.

Bonnie Schlichting

CHAPTER 9

Bring the Whole Tithe

"Bring the whole tithe into the storehouse...
'Test me in this,' says the Lord Almighty,
'and see if I will not throw open the floodgates of heaven
and pour out so much blessing that there will not be room
enough to store it.'"
Malachi 3:10 (New International Version)

While walking in the Adirondack woods in 1984, I realized that my life was in trouble. I had a successful career, but I was drinking and carousing daily. I felt the urge to change. Maybe doing some community board work and increasing my church pledge would be a start. I decided to do both.

Out of the blue, the following January, I was invited to join the board of the largest of Utica's three hospitals. At St. Luke's, board positions were generally filled by people who were the major employers of our community. I joined that board in February. In March, my wife and children staged an intervention and told me to sober up or leave. My reaction was negative, but my friend, Hal, who had been sent away for "the thirty day dry-out," suggested that I try an AA meeting with him.

Wow! Was I ill at ease with *those* people…

After a while, I committed to ninety meetings in ninety days, and I kept that commitment. At one of those meetings, the secretary of my church sat across the table from me. She pulled me aside and said, "You've increased your pledge and are receiving the reward that Malachi described."

Who was Malachi? What was the reward?

I continued to raise my church pledge and managed to accomplish some interesting tasks for St. Luke's despite inter-hospital squabbling that grew each year. In the midst of the squabbling, our board president retired, and after five years on the board, I was elected chairman.

I knew I was over my head and prayed for the Holy Spirit to speak for me. Within thirty days, the Faxton Hospital president asked me if we would merge with them. Wow! That was a dream come true. We merged the hospitals in less than sixty days and went to Albany explaining what we had done. We invited the Catholic hospital to join us, but abortion issues blocked that happening. That was in 1990, way ahead of the hospital consolidations that took place throughout the US.

Whenever I was needing to convince my own board or the merged board to consider the paths we should take,

I asked the Holy Spirit to speak for me, and the words that came out of my mouth were entirely His own.

Merging the two hospitals, we saved the state and our city millions of dollars. In 2013, all three hospitals merged governance, and Utica was recognized as the only major city in NY State to do so. As a reward, Governor Cuomo offered Utica $300,000,000 toward a new state-of-the-art hospital. Ground breaking will begin in 2020.

The Lord of Hosts has opened the windows of heaven and poured out His blessings on our people. I continue to tithe and receive His blessings in my life.

St. John's is one of those blessings.

John Soggs

CHAPTER 10

Dwell on the Good

"Finally, brothers and sisters, whatever is true,
whatever is noble, whatever is right, whatever is pure,
whatever is lovely, whatever is admirable,
if anything is excellent or praiseworthy,
think about such things."
Philippians 4:8 (New International Version)

I was the fourth daughter born to a father who told my mother "no more girls." After I was born, he left.

At seven with a broken back, I moved in with my grandparents, Reverend and Mrs. Robert G. Leetch. My grandfather was a Presbyterian minister. He and my grandmother read me Bible stories and loved me.

At eleven, with my grandfather and the Episcopal Bishop agreeing, I became an Episcopalian. I loved watching grownups kneel at the altar, rather than being served in the pews.

At a meeting of the Episcopal Young People's Association, I met Tony Leigh and fell madly in love. We have been married sixty-six years and rarely missed a church service.

In 1977, we went to Cursillo (a three-day spiritual retreat). Since that time, we have served on twelve teams and begun a new relationship with our Lord. We meet weekly with fellow Cursillistas (Christ followers) and answer three questions:

- How did the Lord speak to you this week?
- What are you studying to know Him better?
- What are you doing to spread His Gospel?

Our travels have been to The Holy Land, The Passion Play in Oberammergau and the British Isles to study C.S. Lewis. In Oberammergau, Tony led a morning prayer group. In gratitude, one of our fellow travelers gifted us an all-expenses-paid week to Andros, the largest island and deepest port in the Caribbean. While we were there, Tony led both worship and Bible study.

We joined St. John's in 1989 and rarely miss a church activity. Together we learned to be Stephen Ministers, office volunteers, and Sunday school teachers. In addition, I served as lay reader, Lay Eucharistic minister, three years as Junior Warden, twenty-five years on Altar Guild, card ministry and now I'm a member of the Order of St. Luke.

When my mother died in 2000, Tony and I donated the Carillons in her name, and now she sings for St. John's and neighbors. Intergenerational companionship and worship enrich our lives!

Ellie Leigh

CHAPTER 11

He Will Not Forsake Us

"The Lord himself goes before you and will be with you;
he will never leave you nor forsake you.
Do not be afraid; do not be discouraged."
Deuteronomy 31:8 (New International Version)

It was June.

We lived on a farm, and as a kid growing up on a farm, I was always on tractors and other equipment with the farm hands. I was almost three, the oldest child in the family, when my mother went in the hospital to have my brother.

One day, however, when Mom was still in the hospital, one of the farm hands rode me around on a tractor and began to touch me in ways he never had before. Then he took me into the field where we'd just planted row after row of potatoes. There wasn't any green foliage yet, just mounds of brown dirt.

Raymond laid me down between two rows of potatoes and had his way with me. I looked up at the beauty of the sky. I didn't understand what was happening to me, but I was very much aware of God's presence.

Raymond stopped working at the farm a short while later. Nobody ever told me why.

Even after Raymond left, my biggest desire was to get off that farm, to get away from those memories, to get away from those fields, to get away from everything that reminded me of Raymond.

Years later, as an adult with grown children, I went back to that place in the potato field. It had become a pasture. I laid down in the same spot. It was still very clear in my mind where it was. I looked up and saw the same sky I'd seen as a child. As I took in its vivid blueness, bright sun and white clouds, God spoke to me.

"I don't like what Raymond did to you," He said. "I don't condone that kind of action, but I gave man free will."

I laughed out loud. It was the laugh of the lame leaping! I'd felt God's presence as a little child, then I'd heard God's voice as an adult. The release I felt was extremely powerful.

Some years later, one Sunday when I'd gone back home to visit, I was at the family church when Raymond's younger brother, Joe, came up to me and said, "Raymond passed."

"Oh, Joe," I said, taking his hand and shaking it, looking him directly in the eye, "I am so sorry."

In that moment, I knew that I had been healed.

The pain from my memories was gone. They no longer had the power to hurt me. The Holy Spirit was so comforting and pleasing, I knew once again that I was in God's presence.

He had not forsaken me when I was almost three, and He has never forsaken me since.

A Grateful Believer

CHAPTER 12

The Doors of Life

"These are the words of him who is holy and true…
What he opens no one can shut,
and what he shuts no one can open."
Revelation 3:7 *(New International Version)*

Doors have opened and closed in my life in ways that only make sense in the context of faith—a faith in God and a belief that things happen for reasons we often don't readily understand.

I wasn't much of a student in school. I wasn't dumb, but I never really cared one way or the other, so when one college accepted my application, my dad suggested that I take it because it might be the only one that would come along (Door #1).

During my first week at college, I met a classmate who became a lifelong friend and opened my mind to public service. Upon graduation, I decided to stay in Dubuque and received my first job (Door #2).

Within five months, I met and fell in love with my future wife Suzanne (Door #3).

In the fall of 1968, at the ripe old age of twenty-two, I was elected to the Iowa House of Representatives (Door #4). Our twin daughters were born in May of 1969, a life changing event in anyone's mind.

By 1972, I'd been elected to the Iowa State Senate, and in 1974, elected to the U. S. House of Representatives. In the fall of 1978, a door slammed in my face when I lost my re-election bid. My wife and I accepted positions in the Carter administration (Door #5).

When Carter lost his re-election bid, within months, Suzanne became the business manager of a community action agency, and I became an administrator at Kirkwood Community College in Cedar Rapids (Door #6).

Later that first year, at the suggestion of friends, we entered the program for the Permanent Diaconate in the Catholic Church. After four years of formation and education, I was ordained (Door #7).

An offer came to head up the economic development program at the Chamber of Commerce in the fall of 1987, opening a door to a new career in public service that lasted twenty-four years (Door #8).

At one point, I felt the call to run for governor—a call that turned out to be a wrong number. Shortly thereafter, two life-altering events changed everything: I was diagnosed with prostate cancer, and Suzanne with early stage Alzheimer's disease. We moved back to Dubuque. Suzanne was offered the job she'd always hoped for, Pastoral Administrator of two Catholic parishes (Door #9).

Within months, her short-term memory worsened significantly. By the end of a year, she had to resign. We moved to take advantage of the medical support services available in Naples (Door #10). I tried to take care of Suzanne myself, but eventually had to place her in an assisted living facility that specialized in memory care where she spent her last three years.

People call Alzheimer's disease "The Long Goodbye." It took eight years for us to say goodbye to our forty-nine years together. As painful as that was, it too led to another door opening (Door #11).

In grief support group, I met a wonderful woman whose husband had died of a different type of dementia a few years earlier. We found mutual comfort in each other's company and gradually found love in each other's arms. This latest door opened to both of us on December 30, 2017 when we were married at St John's.

Our lives are a series of ever-closing, ever-opening doors swung by the hand of God, each an invitation into His Holy Presence. My prayer is that we accept what lies ahead as lovingly as we hope our Creator will accept us at the end of our days.

Michael Blouin

CHAPTER 13

God Showed Up in Publix

***"Call to me, and I will answer you,
and will show you great and hidden things,
which you do not know."***
Jeremiah 33:3 (New Heart English Version)

I'm still learning to sense God's presence. For most of my life, it wasn't something I knew was possible. God was someone distant, who lived "up there." And He was very busy. I was living "down here," and busy with that. But as years progressed, I developed an odd and overwhelming desire to know God, to find Him.

Evidently, He was more aware of that than I knew.

Long before Internet memes were popular, refrigerator magnets were often the source of wisdom. One that was particularly meaningful to me stated *The Lessons I Need To Learn In Life Seem To Find Me.*

But when I realized my deep need to find God, to hear from Him, it wasn't lessons that found me, but blogs and books and articles about the Bible and prayer and God's presence. Not quite the "quail-storm" in Exodus

16:13 and Numbers 11:3, but these things were too often and too timely to be pure coincidence. I wasn't hearing from God—I wouldn't call it that, yet. It was more that I was being guided—okay, shoved—in His direction by His Spirit.

I've been amazed not only that much of what I sought was found for free on the Internet or through free Bible phone apps, but that those books I did pay for were almost always discounted—sometimes only for that day or that week.

The Battle Plan For Prayer is one such gift from the Lord. I was pushing my shopping cart through Publix a few months ago when there was a large, somewhat ugly box sitting in the middle of the aisle near the sushi counter. It was full of books with a sign stating "Discounted." Right on top in the middle of the mess was a brown paperback *The Battle Plan For Prayer*. It was written by the Kendrick brothers, who created the movie *War Room*. I'd just been watching trailers for the movie and reading up on the story. It was the sole copy in the entire bin.

My brain said: *You have a stack of books you haven't read yet. You have cat food to buy.* I pushed my cart forward about five steps and stopped.

A nudge—I don't hear His voice even yet—felt as if it stated: *Go back and get the book. It was put there for you.*

I grabbed my discounted, half-price book and praised the Lord all the way to the check-out line.

God is good. And the lessons He wants me to learn always find me. Even in the sushi aisle in Publix.

Linnea Sinclair Bernadino

CHAPTER 14

The Lord Is My Savior

"…we have fixed our hope on the living God,
who is the Savior of all…"
1 Timothy 4:10 (English Standard Version)

The Lord is my Savior…

We may say those words many times as we seek to live Christian lives, but until we experience Christ in action, understanding His saving grace remains purely hypothetical. Only when we experience Him as our personal savior does the mystery of faith become steadfast in our lives.

When I was a young teenager, the neighborhood I lived in grew to be less safe. The city had hit hard economic times and houses were boarded up. Muggings became a growing concern in the once peaceful neighborhood.

I was walking home alone from my girlfriend's house which was a couple of blocks away. A group of young men across the street started to make inappropriate racial comments about me. I was acutely aware of the

45

uncomfortable situation that might occur. Moving ahead with determination, I prayed for the Lord to help me.

Out of nowhere, a boy from my class appeared by my side. The trash talk stopped from the group. He stayed with me until I was safely home. That was the first time I was frightened in my neighborhood and was so grateful when this person, a boy I barely knew, came to help me.

Years later, my husband became critically ill.

All the medical advancements in the world were not going to cure him. However, through faith and guidance from my pastor, I learned to give the heartache to God. I prayed every day for God to see me through the ordeal of caregiving as my husband grew weaker and spoke less and less.

When the time came for him to die, my husband emerged from his silence and sang *Amazing Grace* two times before making his departure. I truly believe an angel of mercy took him to the Lord.

The same day I had a heart attack.

Through circumstances guided by the hand of God, I was rushed to the hospital and had surgery. I joke that God didn't want me that day—but I was ready to go, for my life as I knew it was over.

Several weeks later, during a grief-stricken moment, I ran a red light and missed a car by inches. Once through the intersection, I pulled to the side of the road and cried. God saved me once again. There is a reason I am alive: I have a purpose in living now with Christ by my side.

The Lord is indeed my Savior...

A Grateful Believer

CHAPTER 15

Humble Yourself

"Humble yourselves before the Lord,
and He will lift you up."
James 4:10 (New International Version)

In November 2014 I was with my wife driving south from Atlanta, beginning our third day of hard driving to the promised land—Naples. I was tired and physically working off the drinks I had had the night before to relax and get some sleep. That was my usual pattern.

Suddenly I noticed we were approaching the cutoff exit at Macon but were in the left lane. With just a quick check on traffic, I pulled across the other two lanes and exited to the blasting of other car horns. What had I done? I could have killed my wife and other innocents. I didn't care about me. I hadn't liked myself for a long time. Drinking the night before was only the tip of the iceberg. I pulled off the road and turned the driving over to my wife. I had to change.

Two days later in Naples I sought help. That was very difficult for me and my ego-driven self-image. Finding

49

the humility to ask for help was only the beginning. I wanted to become the kind of person that God wants me to be. I had to learn to be humble in everything.

"I can do all things through Him who strengthens me" (Philippians 4:13).

I turned my will and my life over to the care of God. That meant letting go of "I want what I want right now" and substituting "Thy will be done." I accepted that I have *real* control *only* over what *I* say and do. With work, I became much better at controlling my attitudes, thoughts, and emotions as well. I stopped fighting anyone and anything, knowing I have no control over other people and situations.

I sought through prayer and meditation to improve my conscious contact with God. That meant starting each day by getting on my knees, praying in gratitude for all my blessings and asking God to free me from the bondage of self and lead me through the day. I always condition my prayers with "Thy will, not mine, be done."

After prayer, I read and meditate on spiritually inspiring materials. One of my favorites is *Forward Day by Day* which is available to each of us in the entrance of St. John's church. In the course of my day, I often find myself saying, "There you go again," hearing Ronald Regan's famous line. Whenever someone says or does something I don't like, I try to pause and pray, then respond, if necessary (often it is not). It isn't easy. It takes a lot of effort to change a lifetime of habits of thinking, feeling and acting.

I found myself mired in the past. I turned to Father Joe for help with my sins and shortcomings. He was very generous with his time. I poured out my heart, welcomed his guidance and, after several meetings, received absolution. The Holy Spirit went right through my heart. I wept deeply. I knew without a doubt that I was forgiven. I even forgave *myself*.

I had a new way of life before me. That feeling of relief and freedom is wonderful. I went on to seek out and apologize to those I had harmed in the past. I gave up my old resentments. Today, I continue with these practices. I try to remain ever vigilant for my negative reactions and thoughts and personal shortcomings. I have learned that in order to love others, I have to be able to love myself. Jesus is now with me on my journey.

In addition to these practices, each week I attend two Bible studies and this beloved St. John's church services. Obviously, I am getting more involved here. I seek to be of service to others in some way every day. Humbling myself daily through these practices has given me a happy, joyous and free life beyond my wildest dreams.

Michael Thomas

CHAPTER 16

A Forceful Presence

"And suddenly
there came a sound from heaven,
as of a rushing mighty wind . . ."
Acts 2:2 (King James Version)

Six weeks before my twentieth birthday, I was getting married.

It was the time in young girls' lives when we'd all graduated and gotten jobs. The next step was getting married. I looked forward to being a wife very much, and was determined to go through with the wedding even after my fiancé's aunt and uncle warned me that it was not a good idea. "Are you sure you should go through with this?" they asked in concern.

As the wedding day approached, my excitement grew. When the day dawned, it was bright and sunny. "You know you don't have to do this, don't you?" my mother said before we went into the church. Maybe I did, but I wasn't backing out.

Right before the ceremony, my dad walked me in the back door of the church. To get to the altar, we had to make a right-hand turn.

When I made that right-hand turn, a forceful wind pushed me back. I knew immediately it was the Holy Spirit, but I wanted so desperately to be married, I tried to convince myself everything would turn out well.

"I can make it work," I repeated to myself as Dad and I made our way down the aisle. I remember little of the wedding ceremony except my debate with the Holy Spirit.

"I can do this," I reasoned. "Just give me a chance. I can. I'll show you. I can. I'll prove it!"

Through all my protestations, the Holy Spirit never wavered. It remained right up in my face.

Nonetheless, I went through with the wedding, and needless to say, the marriage did not work. That made me sad because I thought I would be excommunicated from the church. (I wasn't!)

Years later, when my mother and I discussed my early marriage, I finally told her about being pushed back by a forceful wind.

"I felt it, too," she said in awe. "It took my breath away!"

Joan McCarthy

CHAPTER 17

Thy Will Not Mine

"Thy kingdom come,
Thy will be done in earth,
as it is in heaven."
Matthew 6:10 (King James Version)

When I was six years old, my mom had divorced my father, married my stepfather and moved us to a new neighborhood in Fort Walton Beach, Florida.

Back then, kids walked everywhere, even through the woods, to get to school. One day walking home from school, this big tree said gently, "Child." I had such an overwhelming feeling that I sat down, and I just started having conversations, not even really knowing who I was talking to. It was very comforting, especially at that time of my life when I'd suddenly been pulled away from everything.

Every day after school, I'd sit with this tree, and have these conversations. I have just recently begun to understand—here at St. John's—that voice was the Holy Spirit.

A short time later, I was riding in the car with my mom and I asked, "What's that building?"

"That's a church. A Baptist church," she said.

"Are we Baptist?" I asked.

"Yeah, I guess so," she replied.

"Can I go?" I asked.

"Okay, but you'll have to go by yourself," she told me.

Now, in my mom's defense, she got me up, dressed, and prepared my favorite breakfast—Fruit Loops with no milk—and handed me 10¢ for the offering plate.

At Sunday school, we did lots of arts and crafts while learning about Jesus. I thought it was so much fun! After Sunday school, I went to "Big Church" and sat alone on the back pew, again not really understanding what was going on. There was just this presence around me.

That 10¢ never made it into the offering plate. It became a pack of M&M's from the 7-Eleven across the highway from the church.

At six years old, I had so much freedom and very little parental supervision that it would be a while before I learned the importance of obedience.

Not my will, but Thine.

So, many years later and after my divorce, I headed for Hollywood. I was a trained actor and a member of the Screen Actors Guild, and I just knew Hollywood was waiting for ME!

After four years of waiting tables and getting mostly stand-in work for other actresses, I ran out of money and patience with God. My friend in Naples asked me to help with her parents who suffered from dementia, and so I moved to Naples. Within a year, both of Kim's wonderful parents passed away.

Out of the blue, I received a call from a friend in L.A. whose family was well-known and had connections. He was producing a movie, had a part for me. I could stay at his family's house in Malibu, there was an old 550 SL Mercedes in the garage, the maid knew where the keys were and he'd pick me up at the Naples airport in the family jet.

Hallelujah, Praise the Lord! This is exactly what I wanted!

Two days before he was to pick me up in the family jet, I received a text that there was a family emergency in London, so the plans were postponed. I booked a flight to L.A. anyway.

My three L.A. friends who were to pick me up at the airport backed out at the last minute one by one, and my friend in Naples cried when she brought me to the Fort Myers Airport and said, "You know, you don't have to go."

God tried to stop me, but I wasn't listening.

Back in L.A., I didn't have an audition the entire year. After a particularly rough day at the restaurant where I waited tables in West Hollywood, I decided to walk home.

I found myself sitting on the steps overlooking the La Brea Tar Pits.

Once again I heard a gentle voice say, "Child, are you done yet?" I nodded yes and then a little more firmly I heard, "Then reach into your backpack, past that flask of vodka that I know is in there and pick up your cell phone."

I picked up that 10,000-pound cell phone (you know that feeling!) and made the call to Naples.

People ask me all the time, "If you're an actress, why are you in Naples, God's waiting room?"

And I answer, "I am waiting humbly for His will and His calling on my life."

Tamara Connolly

CHAPTER 18

God's Gift for His Glory

"But by the grace of God I am what I am,
and his grace to me was not without effect."
1 Corinthians 15:10

Critical comments swarmed in my mind long after they took place, never giving me a moment's peace.

Does intelligent thought ever enter your skull? Who do you think you are? You're just a joke with a bad punchline. Work harder, stupid! Never let 'em see you sweat! Don't be such a wuss! You're too fast! Slow down! Watch out! Now everyone's passing you. Hurry up!

When the internal dialogue from the past drowned out external conversations in the present, my "problem" was labeled.

Daydreaming again? Better get with the program. The world will pass you by. Such a space cadet! Earth to Planet Pluto! Come in, please! The truth is simple: you're lazy. You lack motivation. You have trouble focusing. Must be ADD.

With the never-ceasing din in my head, I had difficulty sleeping, but when nothing helped, I decided to act as if everything was copacetic. After all, no one could actually see the war going on in my head. Could they?

They couldn't, but God could.

Through His Word, He said, "Be still and know Who I AM."

"Fat chance of that ever happening," I thought. I'd never get past the "be still" part.

"Empty out all that is not me," He said. "All condemnation. Then fill your mind with Who I Am."

Eternal truth, love, light, peace, joy, goodness, perseverance, patience, hope, humility, mercy, grace, forgiveness, wisdom, understanding, sovereignty, omnipotence, omniscience, adventure, playfulness, immutability, justice, infinitude, sufficiency, creator, sustainer, savior and friend…

"Empty out all that is not you," He said. "All the lies that seek to steal your peace, kill your confidence and destroy your life. Then fill your heart with who I say you are."

Beloved, child of God, forgiven, perfectly and wonderfully made, conceived before time, heir to all goodness, bestowed with every gift in the heavenly realms, joyful, uniquely talented, totally accepted, worthy, purposed, chosen, strong, capable, altogether lovely, cherished, totally free…

I tried to obey. Fifteen minutes at a time. It was difficult. A messy effort at best. Day after day, year after year. My miracle came, not in a dramatic flash like lightning, but in a gradual glorious revelation like the dawn. Nonetheless, it came.

Today, no longer pummeled by the past, I am present to the present, and these days I enjoy being me, for I know that I am God's gift for His glory. The gentle voice I hear in my head now speaks of a rich and abundant life designed in love especially for me.

Thanks be to God.

A Grateful Believer

CHAPTER 19

Open the Door

"Then turning to His disciples, He said privately,
'The eyes that see the things you see are blessed!
For I tell you that many prophets and kings
wanted to see the things you see yet didn't see them;
to hear the things you hear yet didn't hear them.'"
Luke 10: 23-24 (Holman Christian Standard Version)

The Lord has always known me, and I believe I have always known the Lord. The Episcopal Church has been the church of my family for centuries. God is in my blood. But I have not always walked with the Lord.

I was in a pretty bad spot about four years ago. Resigned, cynical, and willing to give in to what amounted to depression, brothers in Christ (all members of St. John's) cared enough to get me help. I took a road trip with Fr. Joe and Leo Velasquez. Leo's wife Iris and son Ruben came, too. We went to the Voice of the Apostles in Nashville.

God had an encounter waiting there for me. One that has changed me and my life forever. I was physically healed. I was spiritually reborn, and I was baptized in

Love. I was loved like never before. The fragrance of Jesus was on me and stayed with me for weeks. I said, "Yes. Yes, Jesus, I love you."

Recently, my wife Barbara and I made a Sunday afternoon ride back to St. John's to deliver altar linens and then to go to the grocery. We had been at church in the morning and into the afternoon. It was after 3 pm, and frankly I did not want to go, but Barbara's invitation had a sweet spirit about it that I could not resist.

Barbara asked to go to a grocery we never use and when we finished she chose the checkout line. The cashier was serving a lady in front of us. Something was not right, though. The cashier kept the conveyor running so if we placed our items on it they would crash into the other customer's groceries. As I watched her, I could see the cashier was quite out of sorts.

When she handed the lady in front of us her receipt, the cashier turned to me. She eyed the case of water I'd set on the edge of the conveyor.

"I wasn't sure if you knew the code for the water, and didn't think you wanted to lift it," I explained.

"Well, you could have asked me before you lifted it," she said sternly. "I could have saved you the effort because I know the code!"

I noticed her hand pressing on her hip and her face compressing in a tight grimace. "You're in pain, aren't you?" I asked. She said yes. Without thinking or pausing I looked into her eyes and said: "In Jesus's name, I command all pain to leave you now." Her eyes widened and her face showed surprise. She asked if I was a pastor and I said no, "I am a believer—a follower of Jesus Christ." She said she was also. I asked her if she knew the cause of her pain, and she said the sciatic nerve. Then I said, "The Blood of Jesus is going to that place now to heal the sciatic nerve and all cells in your body are returning to normal."

She exclaimed that she felt heat in the area where the pain had been. She began smiling. Then she lifted her hand over her head in praise and said loudly, "It's a miracle! Jesus has healed me! Alleluia!" She repeated these words two or three times. The pain was gone and she had full mobility! Tears ran down her face. It was a moment of awe for the Love of Jesus was upon us in a mighty way. Barbara ministered to her and invited her to St. John's when she said she did not have a church.

I went back to the store about ten days later to buy an item and in hopes I would see the cashier again. I did. Her countenance was powerful and her smile was full of joy. Thank you, Jesus!

God blesses me moment to moment. He calls me closer to Him for intimate embraces and conversation. I ask for more, and He delights in my asking. With great joy, the Holy Spirit helps me see and hear things I didn't see or hear before I experienced how much He loves us and wants us to love Jesus and each other. His Love keeps hope alive. His faith in us is trustworthy and leads to life filled with joy.

Mike Johnson

CHAPTER 20

A Gift Beyond Compare

"You saw me before I was born.
Every day of my life was recorded in your book.
Every moment was laid out
before a single day had passed."
Psalm 139:16 (New Living Translation)

In 1957, just out of law school, I was awarded a position with the Department of Justice in a special program set up for honors' law school graduates by the attorney general. Two years into my Washington dream job, I married, and tried to build a marriage while building a career. My young wife was unhappy with the life I'd envisioned for us in D.C., so ultimately I resigned, and we moved to Connecticut.

With a loan and a couple thousand bucks, thinking I was Abraham Lincoln, I opened a law office with a vague idea of getting into politics. I had a political radio talk show, and my law practice was interesting, but I wasn't making any money. Eventually my wife and I were forced to move in with my mother and father. She became pregnant, and we had our first child. I'd quit the best job in the world, effectively closing the door of that opportunity forever. Here I was, struggling to provide for my wife and child and failing to get any headway.

Something had to give.

At Christmas time, during a long walk into the Norwalk countryside, I had a religious experience. I saw my whole life mapped out before me. I'd go back to school, get a legal specialty, and be more than able to support my family. My entire career as a tax attorney evolved from that encounter with God, and I was blessed with both a great career and a wonderful family.

Then, just before Christmas in 1986, tragically and without warning, my wife died. The loss had an enormous impact on us all. My law firm was very gracious. They figured out a lot of places for me to make speeches. I even went to China, but every time I came back to our big house in Connecticut, there was nobody in it. The children were grown, and they'd arrange for us all to get together, but I'd be back in the house, alone, by eight o'clock. That was a very bad time for me.

I didn't want the guys in the office trying to get me dates, but I'd had a very good marriage and deeply wanted to be married again. The vision I'd had in the Norwalk countryside many years before was incomplete. Where was that someone God meant for me to live with the rest of my life? I had no idea.

Kentucky Derby Day was on May 2nd in 1987. A big celebration was to be held at my club. I called up some friends in hopes they'd join me, but they hadn't planned on going. Unbeknownst to me, however, they arranged for someone else to join me—a beautiful woman stylishly dressed in Italian clothes, a widow from North Carolina with a child and a dog. Thank you, God!

That enchanted evening, across a crowded room, I saw the woman the Lord lovingly ordained to be my partner for the rest of my life and complete the vision he'd given me decades before. From that night, Jane and I have been inseparable. In too many more ways than I can mention here, she has been a blessing to every single member of our family. She is a gift beyond compare.

Jack McDermott

CHAPTER 21

Guard Us in All Our Ways

"… he will command his angels concerning you
to guard you in all your ways…"
Psalm 91:11 (English Standard Version)

"No," I told my children. "There could be sink holes out there. It's just not safe!"

Going to the beach was an almost daily ritual when my children were growing up. After all, we did live in Naples, the land of the world's most beautiful beaches (in my estimation at least).

All of my children enjoyed building castles, drawing pictures and sending me little love notes in the sand. Sometimes I'd pack a picnic, spread a cloth and hand out peanut butter and jelly sandwiches, apple slices and juice boxes. We'd munch, merrily watching the waves, until their little eyelids would begin to droop (often, mine, too), and I'd know it was time to bundle them in the van and head home.

In the entranceway to our house, I'd hose them off, dry and wrap them in towels, and hurry them inside, into their pajamas and beds. It would not take long for them to cast off to dreamland.

In the summer, the skies would open as they slept. Fierce storms complete with thunder and lightning would dress the heavens in flamboyant drama, but when the children awoke, they'd find the southwest Florida humidity had lifted, the air fresh, clear and cool, perfect for playing outdoors.

I have so many sweet memories from those idyllic days, but there was one day that was not sweet, the day I made a terrible choice that almost cost me everything.

When I described a new beach I'd read an article about in a local magazine, the children liked the sound of it, so we decided to load up our water wings, inflatable alligator raft, sand toys and other paraphernalia to set out on what we hoped would be our next great adventure.

When we arrived, the children spied a sandbar within sight off the shore. Numerous people walked through the shallows to get there. Whole families even. My older children pleaded to join them, the youngest too young to voice an opinion (that was soon to change).

"No. There could be sink holes out there. It's just not safe," I said, but after about forty-five minutes wherein not one person had fallen into a single sinkhole, I reluctantly agreed. The older children had just learned to swim. I'd hold the little one. We stayed much longer than I had intended. By the time we set off for shore, the beach had cleared off and the tide had come in.

We'd only gone a few yards when the ground suddenly dropped from beneath us. Panicked, all three children clung to me. The harder I tried to keep afloat, the harder it became to keep all four of us above water. I just couldn't do it.

"Dear God!" I prayed when I went under the third time, "I've been a fool! My children are going to die!"

From out of nowhere, a tall blonde middle-aged man appeared. Effortlessly, he pulled every one of us out of the water. As I gasped, he carried the children to shore. I followed him and stumbled onto the sand beside my children. When I looked up to thank the man who had saved us, there was no one there.

Not one single person on that long flat beach for as far as the eye could see.

A Grateful Believer

CHAPTER 22

God Pours Out His Spirit

"In the last days, God says,
I will pour out my Spirit on all people.
Your sons and daughters will prophesy,
your young men will see visions,
your old men will dream dreams."
Acts 2: 17 (New International Version)

It was January, 1972 when I randomly ran into Jim Lovejoy in a grocery store.

We began our friendship when my wife was in the hospital having our third baby. Never one to cook for myself, I ate out often during that time. When Jim heard, he told me he was part of a men's breakfast group, and invited me to come to a breakfast.

"I have a season pass to ski at Mount Mansfield in Stowe, Jim," I said, "so I won't be able to attend a Saturday breakfast."

Well, wouldn't you know that January was absolutely snowless, and snow-making had yet to be invented. Days before the Saturday breakfast, Jim called to ask if I was coming.

"No," I told him, "I'll be skiing."

"But there's no snow," Jim countered.

"Oh yeah," I acknowledged and grudgingly agreed to come. I wasn't happy about it, but I would meet the men at the Holiday Inn in South Burlington on Saturday morning.

The breakfast was three hours long and included all sorts of crazy behavior on the part of the men attending. They were raising their hands and praying! I wasn't impressed and thought they'd either lost their minds or were faking. I couldn't wait to get out of there.

As soon as the meeting ended, I rushed to put on my parka. All of a sudden, five men approached me.

"Wouldn't you like to have the Holy Spirit?" they asked.

I could only stutter in response.

"Raise your hands in the air. Ask the Lord for the Holy Spirit to come," the leader said. All five men laid their hands on me.

BAM! I felt a jolt that left me paralyzed. I was in a state of utter amazement and immobility.

After a half hour, I thought I could drive. I drove home at twenty-five miles an hour. Jim followed to make sure I was okay. At home, I sat on the couch two more hours to recover from the event.

Thank God, I never recovered!

That Saturday prepared me to finally meet Jesus on a Cursillo weekend in 1983. Soon thereafter, I retired from IBM, moved to Naples, Florida, opened a Christian bookstore, and became a member of St. John's.

Perhaps my running into Jim Lovejoy in a grocery store hadn't been so random after all.

Jack Bundy

CHAPTER 23

Every Chapter Better

"He heals the brokenhearted and binds up their wounds."
Psalm 147:3 (New International Version)

From the time I was eight until I was twelve, my grandfather sexually abused me.

For a long time, I was angry with my mother for leaving me with him. As I got older and knew more about abuse, I learned that abusers don't just pop out of nowhere. They've usually been abused themselves.

When my grandfather died, I thought, "Well, at last I don't have to shiver trying to hold it together whenever he's around. It's finally over, and I don't have to deal with it anymore," but it wasn't over, and I still had to deal with it.

For years, I took responsibility for my own abuse. Although I had no idea what I'd done to warrant such vileness, I believed the deadly lie: "I must have done something."

Through years of therapy, the Lord brought me to a place of initial acceptance and forgiveness. When I finally forgave my grandfather, I went to his grave site to tell him.

I said that I was sorry for the abuse he must have gone through to become an abuser. I was sincere. I wondered if my Nan, buried beside him, knew that her husband, a revered citizen and upright role model, was an abuser. When I expressed my sadness for their brokenness that had led to mine, I thought my healing was complete.

But it wasn't.

Years later, my mother gave all us kids pictures featuring our grandfather with his most-prized horse. He'd been an avid raiser of horses much of his adult life. Even then, as a mother with grown children, I didn't know what to do with the picture. I certainly didn't want it hanging on the wall in my home to serve as a daily reminder. Since Mom didn't visit all that often, I decided to shove the picture under the bed in my spare bedroom and to try to forget all about it.

I began to have some really strange feelings. I didn't feel at home in my own home anymore. When a friend recommended that I invite a spiritual discerner, a woman known for healing spiritual unrest, to my house, I took his advice.

As the woman started going through the rooms of my house, she sensed something was wrong. When we reached the spare bedroom, her breathing quickened, and she fell to the floor in obvious distress. Quickly, we helped her out of the room, and her breathing returned to normal.

"I don't know what was in there, but it really hit me hard," she said.

All of a sudden, I remembered my grandfather's picture under the bed. I took it outside and smashed it into tiny pieces. The strange feelings evaporated. I felt a big release and an incredible peace.

For the first time for as long as I could remember, neither I nor my house was at odds.

Even though it took years, I felt that God had finally finished the last chapter and closed the book on my abuse. Today, he is continuing to write a new bold story in my life, a story "which goes on forever in which every chapter is better than the one before (C.S. Lewis)."

A Grateful Believer

CHAPTER 24

Back at Home With God

"For I can do everything through Christ,
who gives me strength."
Philippians 4:13 (New Living Translation)

This is my life's journey.

Beginning at age six through age fifty-five, I suffered from Spinal Meningitis, Polycystic Ovarian Disease, Hepatitis A, B and C, Endometriosis, Uterine and Cervical Cancer, Breast Cancer, broken legs, wrist and hip and knee replacement, Degenerative Disc Disease, Diabetes and Scoliosis of the Spine. I lost both parents in an auto accident, and my baby sister from heart failure when she was only fifty-one. I had three failed marriages. So, I never ask—what's next?

It was my second bout with cancer and my sister's death that really sent me into a tailspin. I went into deep depression. After my sister's death, the depression and pain were just too much, and I turned to substances to ease the pain resulting in a further downward spiral.

On August 8, 2012, a miracle happened. I went to the ER—another failed self-attempt to stop the addictions. But this time, I prayed to God from the bottom of my heart. I surrendered my all to God. I prayed for God to remove my self-will and replace it with his will.

At that moment, my heart palpitated and I was filled with joy. The grief and anger were lifted, replaced with gratitude. My mind was still and I was filled with peace and serenity. The pain throughout my body began to disappear. From that moment on, I have not needed any mind-altering chemical to dull the pain or a walker. It was all gone!

I felt warmth, as if a big mother bird had wrapped its wings around me. Later, my husband, Jack, surmised that was really an angel embracing me. From that moment on I felt back at home with God.

Today my faith is stronger than ever. I know that the power of prayer and the continued support of the St. John's congregation healed me.

That walker that I lived on for four years now hangs on the wall in our garage—waiting for the right time to pay it forward to another sufferer. I am back volunteering at the Children's Museum and Hazelden. I am convinced that there is nothing I cannot accomplish.

The prayers from the members of St. John's helped me keep my head above water until I could swim back to God and surrender my life completely to him.

Life for me is now GRAND!

Thank you to my St. John's family for all your prayers and support. They really, truly worked.

Tona R. Wert

CHAPTER 25

He Has Heard

"Blessed be the LORD
because he has heard the voice of my supplications.
The LORD is my strength and my shield;
my heart trusted in him, and I am helped;
therefore my heart greatly rejoices;
and with my song I will praise him.
Psalm 28:6-7 (Jubilee Bible 2000)

Phil and I met in high school and double-dated initially, then married after I graduated from college (Phil said I moved up into the front seat).

I have a life-time of memories with Phil—adopting our first little girl and celebrating the dual event of her adoption being finalized the day our second little girl was born, finding a 1941 Studebaker in the driveway as a surprise Mother's Day gift that I didn't even know I wanted, two trips to Turkey because I wanted to celebrate my significant birthdays out of the country, the beautiful water-color painting of a sunrise Phil surprised me with and the touching note on the back: "You light up my life."

Phil died just a little over a year after we got the definitive medical diagnosis that he had idiopathic pulmonary fibrosis, for which there is no cure.

We were blessed in that not too much changed in that last year, and he was able to continue much of his routine and we our life together until two weeks before his death. We were able to celebrate fifty-six years of marriage. My constant prayer during that year was that he wouldn't suffer. God answered that prayer beautifully.

God worked in another wonderful way.

Five months before he died, Phil decided WE needed a cat. Phil picked out a tiny kitten from the quartet of rescue kitties our daughter was hand feeding. I got naming rights, and William James In-Trouble became a part of our lives.

As I type this, William James In-Trouble is pushing things off the snack bar counter and trying to walk on the keyboard to let me know he's hungry! He surely doesn't replace Phil, but he does put up with my constant chatter and keeps me laughing (mostly) by living up to his name. The dining room table is covered with aluminum foil and the squirt bottle is always handy to keep him from where he doesn't belong…neither very effective.

Shortly after Phil died, I found a Bible verse on a yellow sticky alongside my daily prayer journal. I don't remember ever before actually finding the passage in my Bible. But there it was, in my own handwriting.

"Blessed be the LORD because He has heard the voice of my supplications. The LORD is my strength and my shield; my heart trusted in Him, and I am helped; therefore my heart greatly rejoices; and with my song I will praise Him" (Psalm 28:6-7 from the Jubilee Bible 2000).

And this morning, opposite today's journal entry, is a yellow sticky with that same verse.

God has brought me through mourning and sadness, and in this journey, there have been countless blessings and daily unbelievable moments of joy!

Blessed be the Lord!

Bonnie Schlichting

CHAPTER 26

Just Lucky

*"Don't you know that you yourselves are God's temple
and that God's Spirit dwells in your midst?"*
1 Corinthians 3:16 (New International Version)

I was lucky to have been born an Episcopalian.

My uncle and cousin were priests. Another cousin married a priest after her brother introduced her to his friend from the seminary. Throughout my early days, I attended St John's Episcopal Church in Sharon, Massachusetts, and I enjoyed it. I served as both an acolyte and a server. When I was young, church occupied a large part of my life.

As an adult, however, I allowed my work to push my church involvement aside.

After working in Boston for ten years and starting a family, I moved to Rochester, NY, to go with Gannett, a newspaper company, just about when the company and corporate office were starting to buy and sell newspapers and TV stations. My wife, Carol, and I had two children, who grew up in Rochester, amid many friends and snow. My career at Gannett worked out very well, thirty-two years and a retirement on Cape Cod and here in Naples. Can't do much better than that.

However, when I was forty-five, I collapsed on a golf course on Cape Cod with a cardiac arrest. My golf partner was a volunteer fireman and started CPR. My son and his friend ran for a phone to call 911. (No cell phones in those days.) A cardiac care nurse from Syracuse, NY (Carol's home town) came from another hole and helped with the CPR, and the firemen used an AED to start my heart going again.

You could say, "I got lucky," for obviously, I survived. Over the following years I've had stents and a heart by-pass as medical science advanced. Even after that I never thought of going to church.

After my retirement, friends Mike and Jean Morley introduced Carol and me to St. John's in 2006 or so. I was reminded of how much I enjoyed and felt comfortable in the Episcopal church, and here at St John's, I was at home again.

When Fr. Joe arrived, he introduced me (and probably many of you) to the good works of the Holy Spirit. So perhaps we are "lucky."

The definition of lucky is "fortunate, favored and blessed."

I now realize, with the weekly help of Fr. Joe, that the Holy Spirit has looked out for me many times, and I thought I was just "lucky!" Well, maybe, I am.

Dick Clapp

CHAPTER 27

The S.W.A.T. Team

"A cheerful heart is good medicine,
but a crushed spirit dries up the bones."
Proverbs 17:22 (New International Version)

Although I've always known that God is with me, I admit that at times, I worry.

Well… maybe it would be more accurate to say, "I tend to be a worrier."

Even more, it would not be inaccurate to say, "I'm a world class worrier." I can't tell you how many times I've read Philippians 4: 6-7 (English Standard Version):

"Do not be anxious about anything, but in everything by prayer and supplication with thanksgiving let your requests be made known to God. And the peace of God, which surpasses all understanding, will guard your hearts and your minds in Christ Jesus."

After taking hold of His peace, I've been known to let it slip right through my fingers and start fretting, first about one thing, then another. When that happens, I imagine God looking down from the heavenlies, shaking

His head and sighing, "Oh, my dear child, there you go again!"

God is patient, and I've given Him a lot of opportunity to prove it, but He doesn't keep a record no matter how many times I slide back into the same old same old (1 Corinthians 13:4-5).

Throughout my life, God's given me plenty of proof that He'll always show up when I need Him, because He always has.

When I recall one particular time He showed up in an especially big way, I still chuckle.

It was around five o'clock rush hour during the peak of "the season" in southwest Florida. I was moving swiftly, traveling west into the late afternoon sun in bumper-to-bumper traffic when without any warning whatsoever, my car suddenly stopped right in the middle of the road.

I was afraid to get out but just as afraid to stay in my car. Listening to cars whizzing past on both sides, I covered my head with both hands and braced for the inevitable impact that never came (Oh, how often in my life have I done that!)

To my surprise, the car behind me did not plough into me. Instead, the driver got out and bravely walked to my window.

"Ma'am?" he said, "Can I help you?" I borrowed his phone and called my daughter; then, he made a call himself.

Within minutes, a man dressed all in black pulled his vehicle off the road near me. Stepping out, he took charge.

I was out of harm's way, my car off the road and towed to be repaired in short order. When the man in black turned to walk away, I laughed when I saw the four letters emblazoned on his back, and I'll never forget that day…

The day God sent in the S.W.A.T. team.

Barbara Youngs

CHAPTER 28

God Is Ever Present

"If we are faithless, he remains faithful, for he cannot disown himself."
2 Timothy 2:13 (New International Version)

All my life, God has been present.

I became a Christian and was baptized in a Baptist church at a very young age partially because I was at the age young people in our congregation were expected to make a statement of faith. But I remember a very important time that I gave my life in its totality to Christ. It was just over a decade ago.

I was involved in a Beth Moore Women's Bible study that took me back through the various stages of my life, looking for God. When I divided my journey into ten-year increments, I found Him in every good time and every bad time in every segment of my life.

In close examination of the times when I didn't feel His presence, I found that without exception, it was I, not He, who'd moved away.

Looking back over the years, I recalled my devastation when I lost my husband Barry. I didn't know how I would go forward without him. I was living in Italy when he died. At first, I considered not coming back to the U. S., but we had a young son, and I felt sure he'd want me to raise our son in the U. S. Before I could arrange to return, however, my father died.

How did I face the loss of the two most important men in my life within months of one another? When I turned to God, He helped me. For a long time, however, I felt certain that I was destined to go on alone. I could not have been more wrong.

I'd been single four years when friends asked me to meet Jack McDermott. He seemed like a great guy, but I still hesitated: I wanted a good marriage or no marriage at all. I prayed and had my friend Joe, an attorney, check him out. After giving Jack a thumb's up, Joe noted the difference in Jack's age and mine, then gave me some advice.

"You either have to marry that guy or let him go. He doesn't have time to mess around!" he said.

Taking Joe's advice, I married Jack over thirty years ago. Our life together has been full of weddings and graduations, births and deaths of people we love, of incredibly happy times and really sad times. God's been with us through it all.

He led us to our Al-Anon and St. John's families when we needed healing for our children, my knee, and my brother with Guillain-Barre. We prayed for a miracle and we got one.

My brother is now the healthiest he's ever been. God provided both the time and the place for my mother and me the last years of her life. He gave me hope and support from St. John's when I faced the illness that Jack's doctors said he would not survive. I'm happy to say that they were wrong.

Having experienced God's love for over seven decades, I know He's always been present in my life, even and perhaps especially, in the times when I moved away.

Jane McDermott

CHAPTER 29

Willing to Stand in the Gap

"I looked for someone… to stand in the gap…"
Ezekiel 22:30-31 (New International Version)

I believe that the ministries God has given us come in all shapes, sizes…and costumes!

Of course, I would, for my name is *Sizzle*, and I am a *clown*!

My other self is named Daphne Pfaff.

For years before she created me, Daphne volunteered as a counselor on a suicide crisis telephone Hotline. As she listened to desperate people at the loneliest, most threatened and despairing times of their lives, Daphne knew she could not help them alone, but she didn't have to, for each time she took a call…

God was on the line.

When we are willing, God will use us to stand in the gap, acting as conduits of His love to those who desperately need it. And like us, the ministries He has given us come in all shapes, sizes…and costumes!

When Daphne created me, it was to minister to people sick in both body and in spirit.

Through me, *Sizzle the clown*, she trained nearly 150 others to clown in the hospitals in our community. Many are faithful people with a desire to minister God to others.

Not unlike crisis Hotline callers, hospital patients are all to some degree afraid, lonely, confused and vulnerable. That is why I teach my clowns to be sensitive, refraining from any coercion toward conversion.

Nonetheless, God is active in every hospital room where we encounter pain and suffering. At such times, we are in fact His messengers, called to stand in the gap between Him and His people to deliver His relief from stress and suffering.

And we are never inhibited from leaving with a hearty and enthusiastic "You're in my prayers!"

We may in humility believe we are unable or unworthy to be one of God's agents of help or change to another soul. But He will find a way to use us…maybe not as a hospital clown or suicide Hotline volunteer but just as positively and just as real if we are open and . . .

Willing to stand in the gap.

Daphne Pfaff AKA Sizzle, the Clown

CHAPTER 30

Tightly-tied Heartstrings

"...My heartstrings throb like harp strings..."
Isaiah 16:12 (The Message)

As I look back on my life, I can see so clearly how God has pulled the strings of my heart to bring me ever closer to His.

Although I had gone to Sunday school at the Christian Science and Congregational churches since I was a child, and continued to participate in young people's groups, I never thought much about my relationship with God until much later.

When I met my husband, Don, in 1949 at Michigan State College, I knew that he had been an Episcopalian all of his life. Because of my former religion, I had never been baptized. I began attending the Episcopal Church with Don. When our daughter Mary Jo was born, God tugged me closer, and after instruction, I was baptized with her, my baby in arms, in 1953.

I was an only child and family has always been very important to me. When I was thirty, Don and I lived in

Detroit near my parents, and we were visiting family in his childhood home town of Ironwood, Michigan along with Don's sister when I received a phone call with heartbreaking news.

My father had died suddenly of a heart attack. He was only fifty-seven.

Detroit is a full day's ride from Ironwood, across the upper peninsula, then south to Detroit and lower Michigan. Don's sister was worried that we would be overtired and have an accident if we attempted to make the trip home without resting. Nonetheless, concerned for my mother's wellbeing, the three of us set out for Detroit immediately.

I prayed to the Lord all the way home.

God heard and answered my prayers. He filled me with a certainty that my father was safely with Him in heaven. The unswerving peace that I experienced through God's assurance drew me closer to Him.

But He had only started to reel me in…

For the last twenty years, I have been a member of St. John's Episcopal Church. Over a decade ago, Father Joe Maiocco III became our rector. Since then, Father Joe has become part of my life and the lives of my friends at the Marbella, the retirement community in which we live. He has visited here once a month for communion and luncheon for the past eight years. Every Christmas, he celebrates with a service for our entire building. He also visits the Cove, our assisted living community, each month.

Father Joe has a way of touching my heart strings as no other minister or priest has done. His sermons and his faithfulness have drawn me tightly to the heart of God. In loving gratitude to our Lord and Father Joe Maiocco, I now rejoice and sing:

"O, come let us adore Him!"

Marilyn Hibbert

CHAPTER 31

Richly Blessed to Richly Bless

"Charge them that are rich in this world,
that they be not high minded,
nor trust in uncertain riches,
but in the living God,
who giveth us richly all things to enjoy;
That they do good, that they be rich in good works,
ready to distribute, willing to communicate."
1 Timothy 6:17-18 (King James Version)

Growing up as a child, my family had so very little.

I had just one pair of shoes. They were plastic, and every time the back would break, my grandmother would sew it back up.

Even though we didn't have much, I was happy.

When you're poor as a child, you don't know what poor is. You know you have a roof over your head, you have clothes, and you have love. That was the most important thing.

My grandmother would always hug me and tell me stories. She did her best to see that we always had something to eat. At times, it was minimal. Sometimes, we didn't have anything at all.

At the end of every day, Grandmother would go to the market and beg for the bits and pieces that had not sold. She'd bring home whatever of the day's leavings she could get and make a meal out of it.

At home with Grandmother, I felt safe, but I still remember what it's like to go to school or out in the community and have people look at you as if you don't belong because you don't have what others have. I grew up with that, but because I knew I was loved, a lot of times what others thought did not matter to me.

Although I am no longer poor, I know what it's like to be without, and that's a gift from God with a divine purpose. Remembering want, I want to help others.

In deep humility and with great gratitude, I give thanks for all that God has given my husband and me through the years. We have been richly blessed so that we are able to richly bless others, all for the glory of God.

Diann Keeys

CHAPTER 32

We Have a Counselor

"I will pray the Father,
and he will give you another Counselor,
to be with you forever, even the Spirit of truth,
whom the world cannot receive,
because it neither sees him nor knows him;
you know him, for he dwells with you,
and will be in you."
John 14:16-17 (Revised Standard Version)

My husband's doctors told him he was not going to survive his latest illness.

Despite their dire predictions, Jack did live, and he was gaining strength in rehabilitation when his doctor made an observation.

"I think you're a little depressed," his doctor said. "I'm going to give you an antidepressant. Just a very small dosage."

Did Jack say, 'Okay'? I wondered in surprise when I heard him mumble.

His doctor must have thought he'd heard Jack give his approval, for he ordered the nurses to start bringing the new medication. A couple of days later, however, when his doctor began to go over his meds again, Jack interrupted him.

"What did you say?" he asked.

"You know," his doctor replied. "That's the little antidepressant I asked you about. You agreed to take it."

"No, no, no, no, no, no!" Jack told him. "There's been a mistake. I did not agree to take it, and I don't want it. You can stop it right now!"

The doctor nodded. He could tell Jack was emphatic about not taking the pill.

"You don't understand," Jack explained. "I have this friend, and when He lived on Earth, He told His disciples that in three days He was going to go away and that He wouldn't see them anymore. But He was going to send them a counselor who would be with them forever. I don't need antidepressants. I have a counselor!"

Jack had been through so much. His body was still very weak, but I sobbed at the sheer strength of his testimony.

"I got it. I understand," the doctor said quietly. "No more antidepressant!"

Through the hard times in his life, my husband has claimed Christ's promise to His disciples at their last supper before His crucifixion. Jesus kept His promise to them then, as He does to us now. He has sent us another Counselor, His Holy Spirit, who will dwell with and in us forever.

Jane McDermott

CHAPTER 33

Strive to Please God

"Your own ears will hear Him.
Right behind you a voice will say,
'This is the way you should go,'
whether to the right or to the left."
Isaiah 30:21 *(New Living Translation)*

I figured I was an adequate, if conventional, Christian. Church on Sunday. Pledged annually. Ate pancakes on Shrove Tuesday. (Even helped cook them!) No spiritual fireworks, but also no thunderous warnings.

I had a satisfactory career in management ending up in the banking business. When the rector heard I was a "banker," his eyes lit up, and I was recruited into parish leadership. (Little did he know, the bank never let me near the money… I was in operations and marketing!) But I was soon on the Finance Committee, Treasurer, indeed Stewardship Chairman. Even got on the Diocesan Finance Committee. I found myself hearing more about, and being asked to preach about *tithing*, and that started to worry me.

I thought I was contributing appropriately. But wasn't I being hypocritical in preaching tithing and not doing it? And ten percent off the top? That's a scary commitment. My conscience (read "LORD," I'm sure) kept pestering, so I decided I needed to give *tithing* a try. If the family faced starvation, I could always back off.

After a while, it dawned on me that I was meeting all the bills with plenty left over. And after that rather pedestrian revelation, I began seeing that there were other unexpected good things happening. Coincidences?

I finally put it together. *There are no coincidences.* What we call "coincidences" are actually God's surprises to encourage us in our choice of direction. As I *tried* to get more in communication with Him and *chose* to follow His lead, I found I received one Godly surprise after another!

A wonderful prayer in *Thoughts in Solitude,* by American Trappist monk, author, theologian and poet Thomas Merton, says:

> *My Lord God, I have no idea where I am going...But I believe that the desire to please you does in fact please you... And I know that if I do this you will lead me by the right road though I may know nothing about it... Therefore I will trust you always... for you are ever with me, and you will never leave me to face my perils alone.*

Merton's insight and all those "coincidences" have convinced me that every time we *strive* to please God, He is pleased, and in response, He sends us surprises to encourage us to continue to choose the paths that bring us closer to Home, closer to Him.

Praise the Lord!

David Pfaff

CHAPTER 34

Faith in God Sustained Us

"Is anyone crying for help?
God is listening, ready to rescue you.
If your heart is broken, you'll find God right there;
if you're kicked in the gut,
he'll help you catch your breath."
Psalm 34:17-18 (The Message)

My dad passed away when I turned fifteen.

His death was not only a traumatic loss for me as a teenager, but also for my mom and my sister, Edna.

Throughout my childhood and into my adolescence, the four of us were a close family who always worshipped together. My relationship with my dad had always been special. We were very close.

Dad was six-feet tall and very healthy before he contracted a serious strep throat infection while in his twenties. The doctors told him his mitral valve was damaged, and his life expectancy would be forty years of age.

Despite his diagnosis, Dad remained vibrant through his late forties, almost a decade beyond what his prognosis predicted.

My sister, Edna, six years older than I, married a man in the army. When they moved to Fort Jackson in Columbia, South Carolina, the three of us keenly felt her absence.

Less than five months later, on November 8, 1958, Mom and I were with Dad when he departed this life at the age of fifty-one.

It was a difficult time. Mom was strong, I was vulnerable, but faith in God sustained us both.

We both focused on my obtaining a college education and worked faithfully toward achieving that goal. With God's help, not only that goal but more were accomplished.

I graduated from Northeastern University in Boston, Massachusetts with a bachelor of science degree in healthcare administration, attended graduate school and went on to have a very successful career. I was able to assist my mom financially over the years.

Through our greatest loss, faith in God kept us focused and even made us happy and successful.

Thomas Sullivan Cinquini

CHAPTER 35

Back to Jag

"Believe on the Lord Jesus Christ,
and thou shalt be saved..."
Acts 16:31 (King James Version)

I was born and raised here in Naples in the River Park Projects.

My mom was in and out of prison, addicted to crack cocaine and heroin. I didn't know my dad. My grandmother had to get me at a very young age. I'd never seen anyone be married in my family. No one raised their children with both the mom and the dad.

When I was about to get married, I asked my fiancé, "Don't we need to go to a church or something?" And he was like, "Uh, okay," so we ended up in a church for marriage counseling with Pastor Williams. The first question he asked was where we were in our walk with Christ.

"I know God, and God knows me," my fiancé said, and I looked at him as if to say, "Oh, really?" First I'd heard about it. When it was my turn, I told the pastor, "I did go to an Easter service once, and I heard something about this man that died...I did hear some story..." I tried to figure out if I did know this guy the pastor was asking about, but I just wasn't sure.

Pastor Williams said, "Well, you can be sure when you leave here today," and he gave us the following illustration: "If you bought a Jaguar and something were to go wrong on it, would you take it to Honda to get it repaired?" That was a no brainer. "No, I'd take it back to Jag," I said. Pastor Williams explained that marriage was like that Jag: God instituted it; He created it and problems are going to come; things are gonna happen. But if you want a successful marriage, you need to have Christ in the middle of it.

I've always wanted to be successful, not like I wanted to be rich and famous, but I wanted to do what I did well. And that's what sold me. God must have told Pastor Williams to re-present Him to me in a way that would catch my heart.

"I want to know Jesus," I said, and I meant it. I didn't know what I was asking for or what the outcome was going to be, but I knew I wanted to be a success, so I ended up saying a prayer inviting Christ to take charge of my life.

Jesus took me up on it, and from that day forward, I've been saved. Now, when I meet people who don't know Jesus, I ask Him to show me how to re-present Him in a way that will catch their hearts. And He's taken me up on that, too, every time.

Shalonda Washington

CHAPTER 36

The Fields Are Ripe

"You know the saying,
'Four months between planting and harvest.'
But I say, wake up and look around.
The fields are already ripe for harvest."
John 4:35 (New Living Translation)

I had been married twenty years before my husband came to the Lord.

He'd grown up in the church, his mother was a pastor, but I didn't even know all that before I married the man. "You need to know people before you marry them," I tell the girls I counsel. I found that out firsthand!

When Jimmy accepted Christ as LORD of his life, he naturally wanted for our family to attend his mother's church in Immokalee. When we did, our kids looked around and then said, "Where are the young people?" When we were invited to visit other churches, they asked the same thing. My goodness, where were the young people? They weren't in the churches.

That got us to thinking. Kids needed the opportunity to get to know Jesus. Easter was coming up, so we decided we were going to put on an Easter production. We put flyers out everywhere. Almost half the projects in Immokalee were there for the first practice, tons of foster kids and kids living in all kinds of makeshift situations.

That was when God began to develop Washington Family Ministries.

In the beginning, the kids had no filter. They cussed the church. If I told them to do something, they'd get mad and cuss me out. If my husband said something, they bulked up like they wanted to fight. I told God, "Oh, nah, I'm not doing this. What do I have to offer these kids?"

All the feelings from my childhood welled up. About my mom being on cocaine, her being locked up, my grandmother having to raise me, my never going to the mall until I was in high school and me just living off Goodlette in River Park. I didn't know what Burger King or McDonald's was, much less Pizza Hut. We lived on beans and greens. My mouth fell open first time I saw the mall.

God answered my question by helping me remember all the people who took me places, showed me things and taught me how to get along in a world I'd lived on the thin edges of my whole life, but never entered into.

"You can do for them what others have done for you. That's what you have to offer them," He told me. But I had a whole lot more: I had Him.

Nothing is an accident where God is concerned, and His timing is impeccable. My business, my faith and my family grew to the point that we were ready to take on ministry. God saved my husband and that sent us to Immokalee. We left the storehouse and went into the fields, and boy were they ripe! It's all God, and it's all good. (That don't mean easy.)

Shalonda Washington

CHAPTER 37

Child of God to Man of God

"I shall not die, but live,
and declare the works of the Lord."
Psalm 118:17 (King James Version)

I know that my Redeemer lives.

I have been blessed with four distinct interventions (or miracles) in my life. Each came at a time of personal powerlessness.

The first happened thirty-seven years ago when the Lord saved me from the slow doom of alcoholism. He put people in my life to show me a new direction while instantly taking away the deadly compulsion to drink.

I had long since abandoned the Catholic faith in which I was raised, and had been adrift. This moment began my slow, but I see now, inevitable return to God.

Years passed as I grew in faith.

Then in 2008, I was diagnosed with stage four tongue cancer. Good doctors entered the picture with their chemo and radiation. After treatment, I attended a healing mission of Nigel Mumford at St. Mary's in Bonita Springs.

I received the laying on of hands and prayers by members of the Order of St. Luke the Physician. Later surgery showed that the suspicious cells remaining after treatment were dead. That was the direct result of their prayers.

Two years ago, I was diagnosed with esophageal cancer. More chemo and radiation. Joan Hunter, during her visit to St. John's, prayed with me and that cancer was cured too.

I finished treatment in January of last year (2018), but nine months later, during a follow-up exam for the esophageal cancer, a tumor was discovered on my pancreas. More chemo and radiation, but the cure occurred during our most recent visit by Judith McNutt.

She prayed with me, and I collapsed from the power and intensity of her prayers. When I recovered, I knew at once that I was cancer-free. Later scans confirmed that fact for others, but I already expected the good results.

I am a Man of God. Judith called me that during her prayers. A first for me! We are often referred to as Children of God, but as a Man of God, I have a different challenge, an anointing if you will, to declare God's love to others. I am a member of the Order of St. Luke now, and each day I lay myself in God's hands and ask only that He put people in my life that I can help and give me the strength to do it.

I surrendered to the love and direction of Jesus, and that has made all the difference. If you want to know more, just ask me. I love to talk.

Jim Bongard

CHAPTER 38

Song of Deliverance

*"You are my hiding place;
you will protect me from trouble
and surround me with songs of deliverance."*
Psalm 32:7 (New International Version)

I experienced God at such a young age that the deacons in the church questioned if I knew what I was doing. I was six when I felt a gentle push and an overpowering unction to go forward and join the church one Sunday.

As my life has transpired, I understood that my coming forward truly was God's doing. I can see why He had me come forth so early in my childhood.

My mom had five girls and one boy. She was a teacher and divorced, but she had a friend. I was his favorite. Being the favorite is important when you're a kid, but then one day when I was ten, I found out what favorite was to him. It was a fearful moment in my life, but God was with me.

My mother's friend reeked of alcohol when he drove me to a wooded area. I can still remember how fast my heart was pounding. "Why are we here?" I asked him. Even though I didn't know why, I knew it wasn't a good thing.

"If you tell anybody about this, I'm going to kill your mom and then I'm going to kill you," he said, opening the glove box and pulling out a gun. I looked around to see how I could escape, but he'd taken me so far out that I didn't know where I was, but I did know one thing—God was with me.

The man pushed me down flat on the seat. When he finally pulled away, he said, "You've done this before." I was too young then to know what he was talking about, but later when I did, I knew that he was so inebriated that night that he thought he had done what he set out to do, but he hadn't. That wasn't a burden that God wanted me to bear.

The man kept trying to get to me, but each time, God protected me. Once, my mom caught the man. She took me and ran. The next day, she called the police. They could arrest the man, but the story would be in the paper and Mom might lose her job. She didn't press charges, and she made me promise not to tell my daddy or granddaddy because they'd kill the man and end up in prison. Worst of all, she stayed in relationship with the man.

The summer I was fourteen, I got a job as a dishwasher at the Hilton Inn. I was excited to be making me some money. One day when I got home from work, my mom said she was taking me to her daddy's. I'd just started my job. I didn't want to go, but she insisted on packing me off to the opposite end of the state. She dropped me at my grandparents' just outside of Tallahassee, then drove back home to Naples to teach summer school the next day.

My grandfather worked out of town during the week. My grandmother was an invalid. Caring for her fell totally to me. It was a very difficult summer. Why had my mother sent me—and only me—away? By the time I got the courage to ask her, I was a married woman with a child of my own on the way. We both cried when she answered my question.

"He said he'd pay me $3,000 for you," she told me. I wondered what all the man had put her through when she returned from Tallahassee without me.

Whenever I'd read or hear stories about girls being molested, brutalized and killed, for a long time I asked why God protected me from those same things.

Through the years, when I developed a heart for helping young people in situations similar to mine, I found a piece of the answer.

Pamela S. Sooknanan

CHAPTER 39

With Me All Along

"For I am convinced
that neither death nor life,
neither angels nor demons,
neither the present nor the future,
nor any powers, neither height nor depth,
nor anything else in all creation,
will be able to separate us from the love of God that is in
Christ Jesus our Lord.
Romans 8:38-39 *(New International Version)*

I was born a questioning prodigal.

Brought up in a strict, conservative Eastern European family that believed in the Bible and read it often, even as a child, I knew many Bible verses by heart.

To me, however, God was like a smiley face sticker up in the sky looking down. He created the heavens and the earth and pronounced them "good." Just religion, nothing personal.

My dream was to break free and live independently in New York City—an impossibility for a young unmarried girl from an Eastern-European family.

When I graduated from high school, my parents were so proud of me they threw a huge party, inviting all our family, friends and neighbors to celebrate.

Hours after the party, I rose before dawn to make my grand escape, leaving a note thanking them for everything, telling them I loved them, but *not* telling them where I was going.

I became a paralegal assistant, enrolled in NYU, got my "I think therefore I am" card, and embarked on a wondrous journey of learning. I was always busy, but I felt empty. Something was missing.

When asked if I had a religious background, I'd say, "Not really," but one of the courses I decided to take at NYU was the philosophies and practices of various religions.

At first, as I sat on velvet cushions, philosophized, and chanted, taking part in the practices of one religion after another, I found each one intriguing, but once the initial infatuation faded, once again I felt the void.

That's when Scripture began to pop up in my head. Repeatedly, "Do you not know that your body is a temple of the Holy Spirit?" made me question what I'd been inviting into my head, my heart, my spirit.

Shortly thereafter, a Christian man entered my life and challenged me to think of God in a different *personal* way. He told me I needed a savior because I was a sinner.

Indignant, I said, "How dare you? I'm a good person!"

Quietly, he replied, "None of us are good. But for Jesus, we're all evil."

I asked him to leave. He did, but he kept coming back, inviting me to church. Tim Keller, an amazing scholar, philosopher and writer, was the pastor at Redeemer Church. Eventually, I began to go.

When I was invited to a Christian concert in a YMCA basement somewhere beyond Bohemia, I went. I cannot remember the song, but it was about Jesus, how He died for us, and how we needed Him because we were all sinners.

Something supernatural happened to me. A switch flipped within me. I could see the ugliness of my sins against the grace of God. I understood all the hurt I'd carelessly and arrogantly inflicted upon others. Humbly, I realized I desperately needed a savior, I needed Jesus. He alone could fill the empty void in my wanton heart.

God was waiting for me in the basement of that YMCA, He'd been with me all along, and He's been with me ever since. I'm blessedly assured that He will be with me always.

Dee Hayes

CHAPTER 40

Joy in the Morning

"Weeping may endure for a night,
but joy comes in the morning."
Psalm 30:5 (King James Version)

"I need to speak to you," my mom told me. "I think you're old enough to understand it now," she continued quietly. I was thirteen.

"You are adopted, but we are family. I am your aunt. You and I are blood, but you and your father are not." Of all the things she could have said, this was the one I least expected.

"Then who are my parents?" I wondered out loud.

"Your real mother's name is Naomi, and she lives in Queens, New York. Your real father is my brother, your uncle Doyle." Wow, I'd just thought that I was his favorite nephew. All my life he'd done special things for me. Now I knew that I wasn't his nephew, I was his *son.*

"When you're older, you need to find Naomi and get to know the other side of your family," Mom said. I promised her I would. "Don't tell your dad," she admonished. "He doesn't want you to know you're adopted." He didn't want any confusion.

My dad was a no-nonsense guy, but I knew I could go to him for anything. Although they were very strict, both my parents always showed me a whole lot of love. They instilled values in me that made me who I am today. I adored them, and they adored me.

I lost Doyle in 2000 and my dad in 2004. As she aged, Mom began to suffer from dementia, so in a way I began to lose her, too.

When I was in my twenties, a half-sister told me that Naomi was dead. When I was in my thirties, an aunt confirmed it. I heard I had a half-brother, but every road I took to find him turned into a dead end.

Years passed.

My wife had a keen interest in ancestry, so when our daughter suggested I buy her a DNA kit for Christmas, I agreed, and I bought myself one as well. Last Thanksgiving, unbeknownst to me, my wife followed my DNA trail and found one of my aunts and one of my cousins.

"I found your family!" she announced excitedly. We gave my cousin a call.

"I'm glad to talk with you," I told her. "It would have been so nice if I could have gotten to know my mother before she passed away."

"Aunt Naomi's not dead," my cousin said. "She's in Queens."

I was astonished.

Within a week, I spoke with my birth mother for the first time. During our conversation, I learned that my brother lives in Palm Coast. We agreed to meet there April 7th. In the intervening months, the two of us exchanged letters, pictures and phone calls.

I'd kept my promise to my mom, and I wanted her to know, but she had developed full dementia. How could she possibly understand?

"Did you see her?" Mom asked when I visited her one Sunday. "The lady's looking for you. You'll meet. You'll see her." No matter how many times I asked, I couldn't find out who the lady was. Could Mom somehow know I'd found my birth mother? Was the lady she was talking about Naomi?

When Mom developed pneumonia, she was put in hospice care. I stayed with her, talking to her through the night before she passed away March 26th. Her wake was April 5th, her funeral April 6th. On April 7th, as we'd planned months before, my wife and I drove to Palm Coast to meet my brother and Naomi.

I buried my mother one day, and I met my mother the next. One chapter closes, another opens through God's orchestration alone.

Rev. Dr. Oliver L. Phipps

CHAPTER 41

All Your Heart's Desire

"Be delighted with the Lord.
Then he will give you all your heart's desires."
Psalm 34:4 *(The Living Bible)*

I was at West Virginia University for summer school when one of my girlfriends invited me to a Tuesday night prayer meeting. When I didn't accept the invitation, she kept on. "Let's go. Let's go. Let's go," she insisted. Halfway through the summer, I agreed.

The first night I went to the Newman Center, the center for Catholic WVU campus ministry, the church was packed by 250 college students in the middle of summer! The church was called Light of Life.

A young man played his guitar at the front of the church. I was so attracted to his peacefulness. Even though I had a solid Christian base, I've always had a churning within me, but as I listened to him play so serenely, I felt at peace myself.

At the end of the prayer meeting, the young man walked down the aisle. When he saw me, he said, "Hi." I said, "Hi," in return, and I never saw him again until school started in the fall. I'd later learn that my *first* night at Light of Life was his *only* night. The center needed a guitar player that Tuesday, and he'd volunteered. I became a regular attendee that summer hoping to see him again. I didn't even know his name.

Although I was in a sorority and already had many friends, I began to make new ones from my involvement with the Newman Center. When Joseph Maiocco (that was his name!) returned to campus that fall, we gravitated toward one another doing things together with a group of on-fire Christians.

On Friday nights, we ministered at Kennedy Youth Center, a low security prison for youthful offenders. We never really dated. We just were friends, but our friendship grew until we both knew it was something special.

Just before spring break, Joe said he thought we should both pray while we were away from one another, asking God to help us discern his will for us. While I went away with my sorority for spring break, Joe went to a monastery!

When we returned to campus to complete the term, Joe asked me what I felt the Lord was telling us to do. "You go first," I told him, holding my breath. He said he felt the Lord was telling us that we're going to be together, that we should commit to each other.

"I believe that, too," I said, releasing my breath and smiling. From that time to this, through many trials and triumphs, we've been a good team. Not perfect, but committed. Committed to one another and to the God who continually gives us all the desires of our hearts.

Janet Maiocco

CHAPTER 42

Wait for the Lord

"I would have been without hope if I had not believed
that I would see the loving-kindness of the Lord
in the land of the living.
Wait for the Lord. Be strong. Let your heart be strong.
Yes, wait for the Lord."
Psalm 27:13-14 (New Life Version)

I was raised in a Christian home. Faith was always a part of who I was. In college, even though I was in a sorority, I was never a crazy partier. If I veered a bit in the wrong direction, my conscience helped turn me back to the right path.

I knew that when I married, I was supposed to be "equally yoked." When I met Joe Maiocco, I knew I'd met my match. Over time, as our relationship developed, we both realized that God meant for us to be together, and we married.

No marriage is without its difficulties. Like in most marriages, my husband and I had to work really hard to get through some things, but in so many ways, I felt as if my life was charmed. Joe became a naval officer. Our first duty station was Hawaii! When we had our son, Joseph Maiocco, IV, I felt certain he was brilliant and far beyond his years!

"How many families get to do all the cool things our family has gotten to do?" I asked myself, feeling grateful.

When we learned that God had blessed us with a set of identical twins, I thought my life could not have been more idyllic. And then we got the news that our girls had special needs.

My first response was to question God. "After following you my whole life, Lord, why have you allowed this to happen to me?"

Then I tried to bargain. if I took our girls to every healing service there was, surely God would cure them of their disability.

When he didn't, my trust and dependence on him had to grow—sometimes with me kicking and screaming, always with lots of prayer! It wasn't easy, but God always came through.

At our parish in Cleveland, people were great with our girls. When we were called to Florida, I was nervous, but I needn't have been. Our girls are treated even greater here in Naples.

Through it all, deep within me I heard, "Just wait. It will get better," and it has.

Today, at thirty-one, our daughters have a place in this world in which to share their own unique personalities and gifts. While Lisa is responsible and goal-oriented,

Lauren is generous and adventurous. They both are givers with hearts for others, particularly those in need.

God used adversity far more than abundance to stretch my faith. While I waited for Him to come through for me, He strengthened my trust in Him until I finally got it: we can trust Him in all things, especially in those we hold most dear.

Janet Maiocco

CHAPTER 43

In His Image

"God said, "Let Us make man in Our image,
according to Our likeness..."
Genesis 1:26a (King James Version)

A little boy about four years old would always come up to me in church. He knew that I had cough drops and stuff in my purse, so he made a point of coming to see what I had that he might want.

One day he came up to me, but instead of asking for what I had in my purse, he grabbed me by the hand, looked intently into my eyes and asked me another question.

"What does God look like?" he said.

"I'm glad you asked," I said. "You know I knew somebody would ask me that one day."

As he watched, I pulled my compact out of my purse and opened it, holding the mirror to his face.

"Look," I said. "Who do you see?"

"Me," he replied.

"That's what God looks like. He created you in His image and in His likeness, so He must look somewhat like you."

"Wow," he whispered, examining himself closely in the mirror.

And then I put the mirror up to me, and leaned over so that he could see my reflection. "He must look somewhat like me, too. Each of us, whoever it is, was made in God's image, so He must look somewhat like them, too. If they're Chinese, African, Mexican. If they're black or white or purple—"

"There are no purple people!' he said.

"Yeah," I agreed, chuckling. Taking the compact from my hand, he held it up to his face again. "Yep, that's what God looks like," I said.

He nodded his head, looked up at me and smiled.

Pamela S. Sooknanan

CHAPTER 44

The Power of Prayer

Are any of you sick?
You should call for the elders of the church
to come and pray over you,
anointing you with oil in the name of the Lord.
Such a prayer offered in faith will heal the sick,
and the Lord will make you well.
And if you have committed any sins,
you will be forgiven."
I James 5:14-15 (New Living Translation)

In the summer of 2008, I was diagnosed with stage four colon cancer.

I had been helping to take care of my dying father, and all the stress of driving back and forth to Sun City Center each week wore on me. When some of my symptoms did not go away and after my father passed on May 5th, I returned to Wisconsin, and after the usual tests, I was diagnosed.

Ten days later, I was on an operating table having sixteen inches of my colon removed. I was then shocked to find out that I had stage four colon cancer, which means it's in the lymph nodes.

These findings resulted in twelve rounds of chemotherapy in a matter of ten months. Plus, I had to wear a chemo "pack" for an extra forty-eight hours of slow infusion. I'd have to undergo both arduous treatments every two weeks.

As soon as I started treatment, I began to go to Wednesday healing prayer. I started my treatment in Wisconsin and finished in Naples. I was very lucky in that "new" Fr. Joe had a Wednesday healing prayer meeting, which I attended every week. This type of prayer opened a whole new door for me in my journey with the Lord.

I truly believe in the power of prayer, and I know that the Lord healed me. As the old saying goes, "He's not finished with you yet."

I am now a member of the Order of St. Luke, and I am praying for others to be healed by our Lord, Jesus Christ. It has become a natural part of my life, and I am truly grateful for what I had to go through to reach this point.

God's peace and blessings to all.

Vickie Bauch

CHAPTER 45

Abundantly Above All

*"Now unto him that is able to do
exceeding abundantly above all that we ask or think,
according to the power that works in us,
to Him be glory in the church by Christ Jesus
to all generations, forever and ever. Amen."*
Ephesians 3:20-21 (New King James Version)

God has always been in my life. As a little girl, I loved church and knew there was a God. When I was nine or ten, my parents went through a tough time, and we didn't go to church as much. I really wanted to go back and I prayed, "Lord, I want to be in your church all the time."

The year I turned thirteen, we returned.

"God, I'm here! I'm back!" I told Him when I walked through the church doors. I gave my life to the Lord that year; at least, I made it official by walking forward and getting baptized.

I think my heart has always been with Him.

When I was in college, I went to school during the day and worked in an insurance company at night, so I was unable to be as involved in church as I'd once been. One time, however, I was able to participate in a youth convention. I was in the balcony looking at a group of children clustered around the pulpit below.

One pretty little girl had a special presence about her. She stood out to me. Spontaneously, I prayed silently, "God, one day I want to have a baby as pretty as she is."

I felt His calm assurance.

At work the following Monday, I and all the other employees were sitting, typing as usual, when the girl on my left stopped, turned to me and said, "Tonya, you're going to have a pretty baby."

I looked at her like, *What?* I'd just prayed that prayer to God. How did she know? When she saw the expression on my face, she said, "Don't worry about it. I get that all the time. God tells me stuff, and I tell people about it."

God had confirmed his promise.

The years progressed, and I married. When my husband, Oliver, and I decided to begin our family, we experienced problems with infertility for three years, and then I had two miscarriages.

What held me together through all our challenges and losses was remembering that God heard my prayer and confirmed His promise. Was He testing my faith? I vowed to remain faithful to His word.

He kept His promise to me and then some. We had a beautiful baby, a girl! Then God blessed us with two more, boys! He always gives "exceeding abundantly above all that we ask or think." Thanks be to God!

Tonya Phipps

CHAPTER 46

Plant a Tiny Mustard Seed

"I tell you this: if you had even a faint spark of faith,
even faith as tiny as a mustard seed,
you could say to this mountain, 'Move from here to there,'
and because of your faith, the mountain would move.
If you had just a sliver of faith,
you would find nothing impossible."
Matthew 17:20 (The Voice)

When my girls were young, we had a neighbor named Andrea. While she had brothers and sisters of her own, they were considerably older, and since Andrea fell in age between my third and fourth daughters, she fit right in with my crew. She loved coming over to our house and hanging out. We often included her in meals and sleepovers, and when her parents went on vacation, Andrea stayed with us for five nights in a row.

The first night after everybody had their baths and were in their pajamas, I started the routine that I did with my own children every night, saying prayers and singing lullabies.

When we all began to pray the Lord's Prayer, Andrea didn't join in.

"I don't know the Lord's Prayer," she said. I was surprised because she was probably seven or eight years old at the time.

"Well, you can have your choice of bowing your head with your hands together and listening or we can teach it to you and then you can say it with us," I told her.

"I'd like to learn it," she said. So that's what we did. Andrea was smart. Within two days, she knew the entire prayer by heart. After that, every time she slept over, we went through the same routine. She always joined right in. It was evident even then that the Lord's Prayer was important to her. "I say it when I'm by myself, too," she told us.

After Andrea and her family had been our neighbors for ten years, they moved away, and we lost touch. Twenty-five years later, I received a letter in the mail with a name on the return address that I didn't recognize.

I opened the letter and read:

"This is Andrea. I'm not sure you remember me, but I was a friend of your children for many years. I'm married now and live in North Carolina.

"When I woke up this morning, I knew I had to write and tell you that I am born-again Christian.

"I am grateful to you for making my life so good because of my belief in God that began when you taught me The Lord's Prayer.

"I just want to thank you from the bottom of my heart."

Since then, when I say the Lord's Prayer, I can't help but think of Andrea and thank our God who takes a tiny mustard seed and makes a mighty tree. It only has to be planted.

Carol Schaller

CHAPTER 47

Fruit of My Womb

For You created my inmost being; You knit me together in
my mother's womb... Your eyes saw my unformed body.
All the days ordained for me were written in Your book
before one of them came to be.
Psalm 139:13,16 (The Evidence Bible)

My husband and I were in Jamaica on vacation, spending time talking with friends one evening when one of them, a medical doctor, began to stare at my neck.

"Don't you see that you have a goiter?" he said.

"Goiter? What's a goiter?" I asked. When he explained, I laughed. "I don't have a goiter. My neck is just fat."

"No, you have a goiter," he insisted. Before we left to return to our home in Michigan, our friend gave me some iodine pills and told me that if they didn't solve the problem, I was to contact my primary physician for testing and additional medication.

When the mass on my neck did not go away, I did consult my doctor. He ordered blood work, but before its results came back, he ordered for me to get radiation treatment at a hospital nearby. Following his instruction, I had the radiation treatment. And then the results of my blood work came back. I was pregnant.

My physician immediately called for my husband and me to come into the office to see him. "We are going to have to terminate this pregnancy because we don't know how much radiation you took in," he told us.

"I'm not ready," I said, but I was shaken. I went home and prayed, "Lord, what should I do?" Immediately the Hail Mary I'd recited as a child came to mind.

"Hail Mary full of Grace, the Lord is with thee. Blessed are thou among women and blessed is the fruit of thy womb Jesus."

"This child is the fruit of my womb," I thought, "a gift from God. I can't abort this child."

When I told my doctor of my decision, he said that if I did not take his medical advice and abort, I had to sign forms legally releasing him and the hospital from any liability.

God's answer to my prayer was clear and irrefutable. Despite my doctor's repeated admonitions, I stood firm and carried my child to term. When our son was born, he was 100% healthy. He's now thirty-six years of age, and he has been a tremendous blessing each and every one of them!

Diann Keeys

CHAPTER 48

Jesus Will Rewrite Your Story

"Everyone who calls on the name of the Lord
will be saved."
Romans 10:13 *(New Living Translation)*

I was in a dark depression.

I could not even go get groceries. I just wanted to smoke my cigarettes and drink my coffee and be in my room. I put dark towels around my windows so that no light could come in.

My family planned out a surprise party for my birthday. In the middle of the party, I turned to my mom and I said, "I'm just completely losing my hope."

Later that night, I was watching TV when Joel Osteen said, "If you want to receive Christ into your heart, just repeat after me," so I did. Then T.D. Jakes came on. He said if you want Christ in your life, just repeat the words that he said, so I did that, too. I'd do anything for God to come into my life and make a change. The last thing I remember before I went to bed was T.D. Jakes saying,

"When God comes, he knocks once. You can't miss it. It's the loudest knock you will ever hear in your life."

At five o'clock the next morning, I was awakened by a knock so loud and so strong that I thought somebody had run their car into my house. At first, I got scared. Then I went to the kitchen, and looked out the window. A star shone on the cross on top of the church next door. I'd never seen a star like that one.

I remembered T.D. Jakes said that when God comes knocking, you have to open that door and invite Him in because He won't come in if you don't. I opened the door to invite Christ into my life, and a wave of fresh air blew over me. My depression lifted and other things started to change as well.

My eighteen-year-old son had a really bad addiction. He was lost. I prayed, "Whatever you got to do, Lord, do it!" Later that day, I got a phone call from the Department of Juvenile Justice. They'd arrested my son. I went to see him.

Although there's generally a period of isolation before detainees are allowed visitors, the lady in charge said, "I just feel it in my heart that I need to let you come in and talk to your son."

When I saw him, my son told me what happened that got him arrested.

"I was at a hotel hanging out in the parking with the guys when the alarm went off three cars down. It was none of us. We weren't even close. When the police officer got there, he sent everybody home, but I stayed and said, 'I need to confess something. I'm on probation. I'm not supposed to be out here.'"

My son didn't even know why he was telling the officer that stuff. He could have gone back in that hotel room and pretended that nothing happened, but something in his heart told him that he needed to tell the truth. As a result, he was sent to juvenile detention for five months.

While he was incarcerated, a minister gave him a Bible. He didn't read it; instead, he put it on the top bunk. Every night before he went to bed that Bible fell from the top bed onto the floor by his feet. He picked it up and put it back, and it would fall again. Finally, he said, "Okay, God, I'll read it." He started reading it and began changing his ways. He turned around.

And that was only the beginning of how Jesus has been rewriting my story since I invited Him into my life.

Marisol Lozano

CHAPTER 49

The Cross on the Hillside

"Where, O death, is your victory?
Where, O death, is your sting?"
1 Corinthians 15:55 (New International Version)

Weary, I picked up my daughter and headed home as my work week drew to an end.

With a nagging head cold, I wanted nothing more than to put my feet up and have a nice hot cup of tea, but I didn't have time to relax. I was throwing a surprise fiftieth birthday party for my friend Jeanette. All our friends would be there.

My husband, Bill, as always, pitched in. Though only seven, our daughter, Mary Elizabeth, did as well. She was already seasoned in event planning, for we made a point of celebrating every season and holiday, birthday and landmark in the lives of our family and friends.

Celebrating Jeanette's birthday was especially important, for she was deep in the trenches of a hard, long-standing war with cancer. We wanted her party to be something special, so we worked hard. Everything was ready when our guests began to arrive.

After the festivities were over, I called to see how my father was doing. He had been admitted to the hospital the Thursday before with a blood clot. My father had a very rough day that Saturday. My mother wanted me to come to Birmingham on Sunday.

Still a bit bleary eyed the following morning, I was driving towards Birmingham just outside of the city on I-20 when a cross on the hillside of a cemetery seemed to leap out toward me, and I distinctly heard the words of I Corinthians 15:55: *"Where, O death, is your victory? Where, O death, is your sting?"*

Instinctively, I knew it was a "say."

My father was the child of first-generation Scottish Americans, and I grew up in a borough in Birmingham thick with Brodies, Gaelic customs and Scottish burrs. For Scotts, a "say" is a telling of what is to come, a premonition with a purpose.

God knew I wasn't prepared for my father to die. He wanted to prepare me by reminding me that death is not the end, but the beginning. I spent that day with my father. He died the next, but thanks be to God, I am more than certain that I will see him again.

Diane Brodie Terry

CHAPTER 50

Grace Upon Grace

"Now I commit you to God and to the word of His grace,
which can build you up and give you an inheritance
among all those who are sanctified."
Acts 20:32 (New International Version)

When I was coming up, every summer there was a
JTPA Summer Youth Program at the River Park projects to
help kids twelve to sixteen from low-income families get
work. They hired me at VoTech to be a secretary four
summers in a row. The VoTech ladies kept asking for me
back.

I had gold teeth, and I was loud, real ghetto
fabulous. Cindy, one of the ladies, would say, "I don't want
to change you. You're beautiful." And every day the ladies
told me they liked my outfit or whatever. One day, Cindy
told me that I was doing great, but I had to learn how to be
tactful.

"Nobody can judge me!" I bristled.

"Oh, no, it's fine. But when you speak loud, people
can look at that as you being angry. We know you're not,"

they'd say. They nurtured me and shaped me, but they proved to me first that they loved me.

Then I got pregnant at fourteen.

I did not say, "What am I going to tell my grandma?" I said, "What am I going to tell these ladies? I have let them down. They believe in me." But when I told them, they didn't turn away; they turned up their love for me and gave me my first sweet taste of grace.

My grandmother did not come to the delivery room, and when I came home with the baby, she went on vacation. She was hurt because she felt like with me it was going to be different. She'd only finished seventh grade and had to work in the fields and such. I was smart. I had drive. I was the one in our family sure to break out of the projects. She was bitterly disappointed.

Now I understand all that, but then, I was just crying, "What am I gonna do with this baby?" I called Cindy, and all my VoTech ladies took shifts coming to help me out. They taught me how to cook my first meal. They showed me how to change the baby and how to make the bottles. They showed me grace upon grace even before I knew who God was.

Shalonda Washington

CHAPTER 51

A Way in the Wilderness

See, I am doing a new thing!
Now it springs up; do you not perceive it?
I am making a way in the wilderness
and streams in the wasteland.
Isaiah 43:19 *(New International Version)*

When I was born, my mom and my dad were not together, so my grandmother pretty much raised me until I was seven years old, and she got murdered. Then I went to live with my mom and my stepdad.

I was not very welcome because I wasn't from his blood. His family called me "the bastard child." The men in my stepfamily chased me and tried to get me alone. When I told, no one believed me. They said I was a liar.

The first time a guy pulled me out of my bedroom window, I escaped. My mom said I'd just dreamed it, go back to sleep. When she saw my pillow thrown to the other side of the camper trailer where we lived, she believed me, but the chasing continued until I was fifteen. That's when I got taken.

One of my dad's sisters saw me get kidnapped and didn't do anything about it. She told everyone that I ran away, and so no one came looking for me. (I didn't know that was why no one came until more than ten years later.)

At every stop sign, the guys asked me, "Do you want to go back home?"

"Please take me back," I begged, but they just laughed at me. The place they took me, people were doing all kinds of dope. From the very first day, the guys told me if I tried to leave or if I told anyone, they'd kill me.

"Do what you gotta do," I told them. My life couldn't be worth much. My own mother wasn't even looking for me. She didn't care. Why should I?

The father of one of my kidnappers found out about it, and asked his son what he was doing.

He said, "I'm not doing nothing. She's my girlfriend."

The father took me back to my mom and my stepdad's trailer and said, "Look, my son took your daughter. They've been going out…"

The whole time his father is telling the lie his son told him, his son's pressing a gun against my back, whispering, "I'll kill your family, burn their trailer, but I'll take you out first."

My mom had all my stuff packed. I started crying and wouldn't let go of her hand, but the guy yanked me back, and she let me go.

For ten years I was held prisoner, beaten, drugged and sold. I still can't talk about most of it. I became a drug addict. (God has since set me free from addiction!) Four of my five children were born into that life.

Most people walking around in the world don't like to think that there are people like me enslaved in their own town. I don't blame them. It's too horrible to think about.

But I am one of a precious few: I got out. It had to be God who helped me because of how many try to do the same thing I did, and don't make it. They get shot. They get killed. God gave me the opportunity to still be here. If it weren't for Him, I'd be dead.

When God called me into ministry, He told me, "Take a good look at all the people out here in the darkness of this world: they've been kidnapped."

Only He can set us free.

Marisol Lozano

CHAPTER 52

More Than Enough

"Yet amid all these things
we are more than conquerors
through Him who has loved us.
For I am convinced that neither death nor life,
neither the lower ranks of evil angels nor the higher,
neither things present nor things future,
nor the forces of nature, nor height nor depth,
nor any other created thing,
will be able to separate us from the love of God
which rests upon us in Christ Jesus our Lord."
Romans 8:37-39 (Weymouth New Testament)

My mother lay on her hospital bed in the dark as I put lotion on her feet. There wasn't much else I could do for her. Thankfully, the morphine dulled the pain in her cancer-ridden body. She was dying.

"That feels good," she told me.

"I'm glad," I replied. I wanted our last moments together to be good ones. A wall erected when I was a child still stood between us—tall and wide and thick—though neither of us acknowledged it.

Ten minutes passed before my mother spoke again.

"Forgive me," she said quietly.

"Whatever for…" I began. But I knew.

"For not stopping them. For letting them hurt you," she said.

Years before when I'd tried to talk to my mother about what was going on, she'd said things like: "I can't take you to the hospital. The police will put him in jail." "Don't bring it up, or you'll cause your father to have a heart attack." "He'll kill your brother." "You're disturbed."

Not only had she not intervened, at times my mother had instigated the abuse by putting me in the line of fire: complaining to my father that I didn't practice scales on the piano, insisting I clean my brother's room…

The old scenes flashed back, but they no longer hurt. As I became an adult, I'd begun to see my mother's fearfulness, to understand her.

"I forgive you," I said, and stopped myself from saying more. The time for all that had long since passed.

"I…I…I didn't love you enough," she whispered.

My mother was telling the truth.

Her fear had kept her from loving me enough to protect me, but she had loved me enough to make sure I went to church, and that's where I met someone whose love is perfect and casts out all fear, whose love is more than enough not only for me, but for all of us.

A Grateful Believer

A Final Word

When Jesus freed a man possessed by a legion of demons that had made his life a living hell, it's easy to understand why the man begged to be allowed to follow Jesus everywhere.

But Jesus told the man that he could not go where He was going. The man's mission lay elsewhere.

"Go and tell everything the Lord has done for you and how merciful He has been," He said.

When the man began to proclaim the great things Jesus had done for him, everyone was amazed (Mark 5).

In Christ's last command on Earth, He gave all of his followers the same mission He gave the man, but He also gave them a promise.

"When the Holy Spirit has come upon you, you will receive power to testify about me with great effect, to the people in Jerusalem, throughout Judea, in Samaria, and to the ends of the earth..."
(Acts 1:8, The Living Bible)

These stories and the people who tell them are dedicated to Jesus.

Made in the USA
Lexington, KY
10 November 2019